"Not exactly a memoir, definitely not a self-help book, more like a journal of a modern pilgrim's labyrinthine progress, *The Beauty of Broken* defies categories and breaks new ground as a raw account of a family that has been through everything—and in the process learned just how amazing grace is."

—PHILIP YANCEY
BEST-SELLING AUTHOR, *WHAT'S SO AMAZING ABOUT GRACE?*

"Elisa Morgan has taken a brave, bold leap of faith and opened up her heart, holding back nothing as she shares her family's journey. At turns painful, joyful, and *always* powerful, Elisa's story offers hope to all of us who know how broken we are and wonder where we fit in God's plan. Here's the encouragement you've been looking for!"

—LIZ CURTIS HIGGS
BEST-SELLING AUTHOR, *BAD GIRLS OF THE BIBLE*

"I know firsthand the wounds of a broken family. In fact, if we are honest, all of us come from families that are broken in some way. I'm grateful for this book that takes us on a path to see that there is nothing in our past or present so broken that God can't redeem it. God turns the broken into the beautiful."

—RICH STEARNS
PRESIDENT, WORLD VISION US
AUTHOR, *UNFINISHED: BELIEVING IS ONLY THE BEGINNING*

"*The Beauty of Broken* is a page-turner that sings hope in the minor key. Elisa Morgan has poured her heart onto these pages, sharing her tragic and triumphant journey with breathtaking honesty. For anyone facing the unique heartbreak of having to surrender what feels like a part of yourself, this book is a must read."

—CAROL KENT
SPEAKER AND AUTHOR, *WHEN I LAY MY ISAAC DOWN*

"Elisa Morgan has written a soul-stirring, heart-rending, and hope-producing account of her interior world. She, in the tradition of Brennan Manning, draws the curtain of her life and invites us to see her broken heart pieces slowly being reshaped, mended, and made beautiful. She, by example, encourages us to recognize the need to discard the compulsive desire to present a perfect image to the public while languishing in the messiness of the private. Elisa's refreshing candor and genuine reflection of God's perpetual provision for his children is a sweet touch of Jesus for every reader who chooses it."

—MARILYN MEBERG
AUTHOR, *CONSTANTLY CRAVING*
SPEAKER WITH WOMEN OF FAITH

"There are an infinite number of ways we experience brokenness, and just as many responses to it. In *The Beauty of Broken*, Elisa has chosen to tackle her personal brokenness head-on, with an honest vulnerability that both comforts and inspires. She is a wonderful example of allowing God to use the hard stuff and pain in our lives to shape us for his glory and service."

—DR. WESS STAFFORD
PRESIDENT AND CEO, COMPASSION INTERNATIONAL

"The church today is desperately thirsty for the message Elisa Morgan shares so powerfully. And with such long-standing credibility as a champion of healthy families, she's exactly the person we trust to share it with us. Her transparency and truth telling are both disarming and life giving. With piercing grace and playful eloquence, Morgan exposes the destructive myth of the *perfect family*. The lying hiss silenced, Morgan creates space for readers to hear the gracious voice of God in the midst of our brokenness."

—MARGOT STARBUCK
AUTHOR, *THE GIRL IN THE ORANGE DRESS*

"With courage and candor, Elisa Morgan opens the closets of her life, laying bare the messiness of parenting, marriage, and relationships with aging parents and relatives. Honest in her struggles, Morgan takes you deep into her experiences as she learns to relinquish fixing the embarrassing flaws of loved ones, to love her children when they choose mysterious paths that clash with her Christian values, and to trust God to reform not only herself but her loved ones through their brokenness. I recommend this enthralling book to anyone who is broken, and that's all of us."

—Dr. Sue Edwards
Professor at Dallas Theological Seminary
Author, DiscoverTogetherSeries.com

"Elisa Morgan is a storyteller in the true sense of the word. She has a way of taking big ideas, breaking them down, and turning them into helpful, tangible tools. As she weaves her personal stories, life lessons, and teachings together you'll be astonished at how quickly she's shared true wisdom with you that can really impact your life."

—Sandi Patty
Grammy and Dove Award-winning singer

"With passion and piercing honesty, Elisa Morgan builds the case that being broken in a family isn't bad—it's our unlikely way back to God if we surrender our shattered hearts and embrace his divine journey. A strong and brave book. A stirring and inspiring family story."

—Patricia Raybon
Author, I Told the Mountain to Move and My First White Friend

"It's time we stopped confusing what it means to walk with Jesus with the American Dream and got over the illusion that being a Christian guarantees us a perfect family. We are all broken. Elisa Morgan has courageously done us all a favor by telling her own story to make that very point. This is realism, but not at the expense of hope. Again and again, her story reminds us that God is at work with deep purpose in the places where we feel the greatest loss."

—Carolyn Custis James
Author, Half the Church: Recapturing God's Global Vision for Women

"Before Jesus died for us he suffered with us. His soul was steeped in brokenness long before the spear pierced his ribs and the nails penetrated his hands. And he was beautiful. Elisa Morgan tells the story of how this beauty found its way through the cracks and crevices of her brokenness. She transparently shares her pain, loss, confusion, and yes, hope, so that those of us who find ourselves following in her footsteps might find stepping stones of faith to walk on toward the beauty."

—JIM HENDERSON
AUTHOR, *JIM & CASPER GO TO CHURCH*
CEO, JIM HENDERSON PRESENTS

"I love how redemptive God is—I never get over his willingness and ability to take hurt and pain and brokenness into beauty and grace. He has done that with Elisa Morgan. She tells her story with that same beauty and grace, with tender vulnerability and brutal honesty. You will be blessed."

—JUDY DOUGLASS
AUTHOR, SPEAKER, ENCOURAGER
DIRECTOR OF WOMEN'S RESOURCES, CRU

"A brave and beautiful story that takes on the status quo expectations of those in the 'public eye.' Elisa's honesty will draw you in, challenge you, move you, convict you, and ultimately leave you feeling known and loved."

—SHAYNE MOORE
AUTHOR, *GLOBAL SOCCER MOM* AND *REFUSE TO DO NOTHING*

"Elisa Morgan will no doubt help mend many broken lives by sharing her secret journey. I laughed out loud and cried as well while reading *The Beauty of Broken*. I pray that through Elisa's wisdom and example, women far and wide will ignore the tug to put up false fronts to please the world around them. I also pray that God continues to loosen the bricks in my wall so that someday they are simply gone and I can be free to just be who God made me to be."

—LORI RHODES
NATIONAL FOUNDER, CHICKTIME

"Let's face it—every family is a little dysfunctional. But rather than trying to fix or forget our past, Elisa Morgan invites us to dive in and discover just what God can teach us in and through the broken places of our lives. With bold candor and tender vulnerability, Elisa leads us to embrace the joy and pain of life in family and reveals her own deep and hard-won faith. You will not be able to put this one down, and you'll want to pass it along to every woman you know who wants to understand herself and her family."

—NICOLE UNICE
MINISTRY LEADER, NATIONAL SPEAKER, COUNSELOR
AUTHOR, *SHE'S GOT ISSUES*

"Elisa Morgan's transparency is transforming. Yes, for Elisa, but also for the reader. Her raw struggles touch deep places in our lives, and we travel vicariously to a new place of understanding and potential healing. Not only do we all come from broken families but biblical families are also broken. God's family is broken. Elisa's work propels us to the hopeful place of acknowledging this, and in the process we see true beauty in the brokenness—even when the story is still ongoing."

—DR. BEV HISLOP
PROFESSOR OF PASTORAL CARE AT WESTERN SEMINARY, PORTLAND, OREGON
AUTHOR, *SHEPHERDING WOMEN IN PAIN* AND *SHEPHERDING A WOMAN'S HEART*

"Reading this 'work of heart' reminded me of my first encounter with a stained glass window. It's only when we press our faces up close that we realize that this stunningly beautiful thing that we're beholding is actually composed of thousands of broken pieces. Such is the case with all of our lives, and kudos to my friend Elisa for so eloquently calling our attention to this fact and helping us realize that we are not alone. I'll be recommending this book to every client who struggles with family brokenness—which is to say, all of them."

—SHANNON ETHRIDGE, MA
CERTIFIED LIFE COACH AND INTERNATIONAL SPEAKER
BEST-SELLING AUTHOR OF TWENTY BOOKS, INCLUDING THE
EVERY WOMAN'S BATTLE SERIES

"Everyone has stories—the ones they tell and the ones they lived. The pain from a broken home is real. I know. I also come from a broken home. In looking back we see God's goodness and his grand plan. Elisa Morgan risks opening her heart in sharing the pain and the healing over which she had little control. Out of the hurts of her battle, God reveals his greater good. *The Beauty of Broken* will warm your heart and help you heal."

—Jerry E. White, PhD
Major General, USAF, Ret.
International president emeritus, The Navigators

"Elisa Morgan takes you on a poignant tour of her life, shining light on the darkest corners and opening the closets most would prefer to keep locked—*forever*. Be prepared to discover a brokenness, which feels undeniably familiar and painfully close to home. Go there with her, and just like me, you'll be reminded that it's in our most desperate moments that we confront the most beautiful truth. There's *nothing* in life and *nothing* we could ever do that is beyond the reach of grace. In our broken lives, his glory is revealed."

—Tami Heim
President and CEO, Christian Leadership Alliance

"LOVE, LOVE, LOVE *The Beauty of Broken*! Leave it to Elisa, in a *Glass Castle* sort of way, to love and encourage those around her as she paves the road to authentic living by openly revealing her not-so-perfect story. Elisa shares the good, the bad, and the ugly, sprinkles it all with humor, and clearly points to biblical truth. Her welcome candor buttressed by the revelation of Christ's kind love and sufficiency just might encourage the same open dialogue in our own lives."

—Kay Wills Wyma
Author of *Cleaning House: A Mom's Twelve-Month Experiment to Rid Her Home of Youth Entitlement*

"In *The Beauty of Broken*, Elisa Morgan has pulled back the covers of her life to give hope to all who live in and through brokenness. Her willingness to be vulnerable has created a new space in my heart for the possibility that our vulnerability with others will allow us to see God's redemption in new ways."

—Phyllis Hendry
President and CEO, Lead Like Jesus

"Elisa Morgan's premise is simple: *There is no such thing as a perfect family*. What's complicated is how any of us deals with the imperfections in our parents, our children, our spouses, and ourselves. With remarkable vulnerability, Elisa exposes her own family's struggles so that she can help others deal with family challenges in light of God's grace."

—Dale Hanson Bourke
Author, *Embracing Your Second Calling* and The Skeptic's Guide series

"Raw, tender, honest, and unwavering, Elisa Morgan does more than open her heart; she allows her vulnerability to be a connecting point to the pain we all share. She willingly lays before us the difficult truth of her own story in a way that drives us back into our own stories. She gives us sacred space not only to admit that we are all broken but to do the audacious and unthinkable—to consider the beauty of that brokenness. This book will minister to every heart that is willing to deal honestly with the shattered pieces of our not-so-perfect lives and allow God's sweet Spirit to heal, to humble, and to transform."

—R. Scott Rodin
Author and speaker

"Elisa Morgan shares her secrets and in the process reveals ours too: broken people create broken families. Not only is that a relief—it is truly good news. *The Beauty of Broken*—helpful . . . hopeful . . . healing!"

—Robert Gelinas
Elisa's Pastor, Colorado Community Church
Author, *The Mercy Prayer*

"There are few women whose own family stories have been under scrutiny the way Elisa Morgan's have been. Her bold courage to 'tell it all' must come with a bit of fear and trembling as she bares the deepest joy and muck and sorrow of her broken stories and God's healing work in them. With great passion she gently opens the conversation for us all to admit that this is our story too. I ached and hoped my way through these pages and am desperate for others to do the same. I believe this book will open hearts and change lives, and I dare you to read it! Her words are beautiful and wise, her insight is timeless, and her hope is unyielding."

—Tracey Bianchi
Writer and speaker
Pastor, Christ Church of Oak Brook

"We are all broken, thus, we all need God. Unfortunately, my pride keeps me from that desperate dependence on God. Elisa's transparency around her brokenness reminds us that our relationship with God does not require perfection but requires us to desire him. We must humble ourselves and let go of our pride. God simply promises us himself. A wonderful read."

—Diane Paddison
Author, *Work, Love, Pray*
Founder, 4word, www.4wordwomen.org

"I coauthored several books with Elisa when we worked together at MOPS International, and I walked through many of these life experiences with her. Now, as she shares them for the first time, she takes our faith to a place of authenticity that is contagious. We, too, can be courageous enough to admit our brokenness, especially in our relationships with those we love the most, and receive a new kind of freedom in God's astonishing grace."

—Carol Kuykendall
Speaker, Author, friend

The Beauty
of Broken

The Beauty of Broken

My Story, and Likely Yours Too

Elisa Morgan

W PUBLISHING GROUP

AN IMPRINT OF THOMAS NELSON

Published in Nashville, Tennessee, by W Publishing Group. W Publishing is a registered trademark of Thomas Nelson, Inc.

Published in association with Alive Communications, Inc., 7680 Goddard Street, Suite 200, Colorado Springs, CO 80920. www.alivecommunications.com

Thomas Nelson, Inc., titles may be purchased in bulk for educational, business, fund-raising, or sales promotional use. For information, please e-mail SpecialMarkets@ ThomasNelson.com.

Library of Congress Cataloging-in-Publication Data

Morgan, Elisa, 1955-
  The beauty of broken : my story, and likely yours too / Elisa Morgan.
    pages cm
  Includes bibliographical references.
  ISBN 978-0-8499-6488-6 (trade paper)
  1. Morgan, Elisa, 1955- 2. Christian biography--United States. I. Title.
  BR1725.M5295A3 2013
  277.3'082092--dc23
  [B]   2013003344

Printed in the United States of America

15 16 17 RRD 6

To my first and second families, with gratefulness for all we have become both individually and together.

This is *my* story.
This is not Evan's story.
This is not Eva's story.
This is not Ethan's story.
It is not the story of my father, mother, sister, or brother,
or anyone else in my family.
So please don't judge any of them by these pages.
This is *my* story, as I believe God wants me to tell it.
And maybe—just maybe—it's your story too.

Contents

Part Three: The Beauty of Broken

It's Time to Talk

Maybe you know me as the former president of MOPS (Mothers of Preschoolers) International. Maybe that's why you picked up this book—to read what I have to say about mothering and family.

Well, there is that part of me.

Maybe you've never heard of me and you picked up this book because of its title, because of the image on the cover, or because it was on sale.

It could be that someone gave this to you and pretty much just told you to start reading.

Whatever motivated you to open to this page, I'm glad you're here. This is what I want you to know as you turn the pages:

For twenty-something years I had the privilege of leading an international nonprofit ministry, reaching over a million moms in that season. I still believe the promise that "better moms make a better world." (Not perfect moms . . . just *better* moms.) Over those years of leading a staff to lead a constituency, I stood on platforms and worked to integrate the private Elisa with the public Elisa while obediently yielding both "me's" to the organizational mission of MOPS International.

But a large slice of Elisa was silent during that long season.

The mother and more. The other-than-mother. The woman-child. The survivor. The person on a path walking closely with God while scratching her head at what he allows into life. The pilgrim in progress. The rest of me.

I certainly gave much of myself in those years—serving as a kind of poster child for the movement of moms. But some things I couldn't share. Within the walls of my home, behind the face of the leader and in the heart of the mother, were the normal trials and struggles of a woman finding her way. And there were the issues of others who lived with me. While their choices affected me, and my response to them created more layers of my own story, they did not *belong* to me. I kept these situations private as our family hunkered down to survive several seasons that stretched into our new normal. I was not alone in this tempest. In each stage of my family life, I was supported and guided by my husband, our pastor, our extended family, faithful and honest friends, and the board and leadership of MOPS International.

There's wisdom in applying duct tape to our mouths in suffering seasons. In the raw reality of pain, we do well to sit in silence. But it can also be dangerous to be quiet for too long. Frederick Buechner observes in *Telling Secrets*, "It is important to tell at least from time to time the secret of who we truly and fully are—even if we tell it only to ourselves—because otherwise we run the risk of losing track of who we truly and fully are and little by little come to accept instead the highly edited version which we put forth in hope that the world will find it more acceptable than the real thing."[1]

My journey has been stunningly rewarding, wrenchingly painful, and unavoidably revealing. I've sat in

- counseling rooms,
- hospital rooms,
- courtrooms,

- waiting rooms, and
- inmate visitation rooms.

Many issues have entered our home: alcoholism, learning disabilities, legal issues, abortion, homosexuality, addiction, teen pregnancy, infertility, adoption, divorce, and death.

Surprised? I was shocked. But then, I suppose Adam and Eve were, too, over Cain and Abel. And Noah, Abraham, Leah, and King David. The list goes on. We are all broken. Humankind broke apart from our one true and perfect Parent and has been breaking away ever since.

It's time to talk. To share the layers of learning as a woman. To reveal more of me: the public and the private. The mess of a mother saved by grace and loved by God, re-formed into a new version of Elisa. The things I tried that worked, and the many attempts that didn't. What I'm glad I did and what I wish I'd done. The confidence and the confusion. The woman-child learning to *live loved* by God and inviting others to do the same. It's time to tell my story so that you will know there are others like you. So that you know you are not alone. That my story is likely yours too.

There's another reason I'm ready to write. I can finally *see*. From the vantage point of survival, I can look back and take in moment after moment of the presence of God in my story. Sure, I saw some facets of his being as we lived it out. I likely would have not made it to now if I hadn't. But today, I can see *more*. There's a responsibility in that seeing: telling. The truth, Jesus said, will set us free—and there are many who are desperately in need of being set free from the guilt and confusion of the myth of the perfect family that pervades our Christian culture. Lord knows I needed to be.

Today I own it: I bought into this myth. I honestly believed that if I implemented "perfect family values," then I would have a perfect family. I had good reason to attempt this methodology: a desire to repair my own original broken family and create a better product in my second. But looking back, I can see the blind smugness I carried without even knowing it. I embraced the mantra: "Read the Bible, pray, teach kids about the Lord, and they will be paragons of Christian virtue." Oh, how I wanted the promised results!

Didn't work out that way.

Are you exhausted by this fairy tale? Sick of it? How did we become convinced that following Jesus would provide an escape from sorrow in our families, that discipleship would always produce loyal disciples? And why do we keep pursuing the myth that if we just follow some parenting formula, our children, even the wayward ones, will turn out right?

Formulaic promises about the family may have originated in well-meaning intentions, but such thinking isn't realistic. It's not helpful. It's not even kind—this prodding one another to think we can create something we can't: families immune from breakage. Brennan Manning shatters our self-protective facades with his piercing truth: "Living out of the false self creates a compulsive desire to present a perfect image to the public so that everybody will admire us and nobody will know us."[2] Ugh.

Like me, don't you lean out hard, looking for some other kind of hope? *Real* hope—the kind that stays up into the wee hours to sit and watch with you?

I've come to discover that God offers such hope in the form of "*broken* family values"—values for our messy, imperfect families—so that we might remain in relationship with him. He understands that no one is perfect. He knows the unique journeys of loved ones. He gets it that abnormal is actually pretty normal. That people mess up and yet are worthy of respect and love and are never—ever—without hope. God holds each family close, crying with his wounded children, tenderly assembling and reassembling fallen fragments, creating us into better versions of ourselves.

I have to admit, I'm a bit terrified. I realize as I write, telling you my broken story, that I risk disappointing you. You may or may not like me in the end. In order to offer the rest of me and the insights I now hold dear, I'm giving up control over what you think of me.

Hopefully, you'll find a friend in me. You'll discover that while you thought you were the only one, you're not.

Okay. So be it. Here goes . . .

Part One

BROKEN US

Ring-a-round a rosie,
A pocket full of posies,
Ashes! Ashes!
We all fall down.

—Traditional nursery rhyme[1]

We do not want to embark on a further journey if it feels like
going down, especially after we have put so much sound and
fury into going up.

—Richard Rohr[2]

1

I Come from a Broken Family

When I was five, my father sat in a white upholstered chair in his home office and told me we needed to have a chat. I loved my daddy, and daddy time was rare—so I scrambled atop his legs as they stretched out on the ottoman before him. He put his hands on my scrawny shoulders, looked into my eyes, and stunned me with his words. "Elisa, I've decided I don't love your mother anymore. We are getting a divorce."

In that moment my family fell and broke. I wondered what I had done to break it and what I could do to fix it.

My fractured family—my mother, sister, brother, and I—moved across the continent to the hills outside of San Francisco. I'm not sure why Mother moved us so far away. Earlier in their marriage, I'd been born there. Perhaps it held memories of happiness she hoped to reclaim. In any case, we lived in the 'burbs and Mother worked in the city, driving the dramatic span of the Golden Gate Bridge there and back each day.

A peek at her pedigree revealed that Paige, my mother, was

the adventurous type. After she survived polio as a seven-year-old, it's no wonder her parents doted on her as their precious, gifted child. She went off to college, double-majoring in mathematics and airline administration. (There were airlines then?) From her home in Texas, she moved to New York City, where she worked for the C. E. Hooper Company—the company that invented the earliest television ratings system. A single girl doing single things in the big time. Eventually she hosted her own radio and television shows back in Texas, where she met and married my father and then settled down to housewifery. It wasn't a role that suited my ambitious mother, and soon she began to lose herself in the husband-focused era of the 1950s.

After the divorce, my mother courageously returned her attention to her career, but her heart wasn't in it. Or maybe her heart wasn't whole enough to invest it anywhere after the rejection of my father. Instead of receiving joy from her work, Paige began a long decline.

For me, those fun and free early-elementary years were filled with ballet and Girl Scouts and hours of make-believe. One of my favorite imaginings was the Old West, where I would gallop around in our yard on my broomstick pony, gathering mimosa pods, and then squat to crush their seeds into a pulpy pretend food, mimicking what I imagined about Native American life. I'd tie long garden stakes together at one end to become the form for a teepee and cover them with an old bedspread. Or I'd take my plastic horse collection out to the flower beds, where I'd prance them about under what I imagined to be sequoia-sized azalea bushes.

Aside from the shattering announcement made by our principal over the loudspeaker that President John F. Kennedy had been assassinated, and the repeat act against his brother Robert a few years later, I remember this season as "happy with a hole."

About every six months my father visited from Florida, where he'd transferred with his "now" family of a new wife and her daughter. We'd *so* been replaced. My baby brother was too young to accompany us out to dinner. So it was always just my sister, Cathy, two years older, and me—along with my father's new wife, now our stepmother. I kinda hated her. No, I did hate her. She'd stolen my father from me. In twin petticoated dresses with matching black patent leather shoes, my sister and I would wait at the front window until his Cadillac pulled in the drive and the dog barked his arrival. All the excitement of seeing Daddy twisted into turmoil as we sat in grown-up, fancy restaurants and tried to cut through the awkward silence, lumped up emotions, and well-done steaks with knives we could barely manage.

As far as I could tell in those early years, Mother kept all the balls in the air. In fact, in typical Paige flair she went way beyond the norm in many instances. There was always food in our pantry, but she rebelled against everyday cuisine and instead offered us dishes like "Weenies in a Cloud" (a casserole created from cut-up hot dogs, mashed potatoes, and Velveeta) and "Petit Morceau" (after consulting her French dictionary, Mother christened "scrap stew" with this fancy title). There were always clothes in our closet. Often matching clothes for my sister and me, but also some fun items. I remember muu-muus brought back from our grandparents' trip to Hawaii. We called Mother's parents Munna and Bop, and they pronounced *Hawaii* "Hawaya."

Mother embraced our need for a dog with a black cocker spaniel named Lacy—whom we all discovered was pregnant when she pawed at the door, crouched the second she hit the patio, and then raced around the yard, trailing a tiny puppy still attached to the umbilical cord that attached to the placenta that was still inside her. Of course at the moment I didn't know such things existed. It just looked to me that Lacy had pooped a puppy and ran from it, appalled.

Even if she was a bit unusual in some ways—Mother insisted on giving out apples and raisins at Halloween because "children needed a healthy alternative to candy" (*how embarrassing!*)— she brought all the holidays to life. Christmas morning was a department store window display of toys for each of us. Our birthdays were celebrated with a homemade cake *and* a party— like the dress-up bridge party where we all wore our moms' old ball gowns. And to her credit, she fostered our relationships with our two older half brothers from my father's first marriage to the degree that they became safe harbors for us in the tumultuous years of trying to make sense of our broken family reality.

Looking back, though, I can *feel* her weariness. She spent evenings in her chair or on the couch, smoke circling up from her cigarette, condensation forming on her ever-present highball of Scotch. Her bathroom shower remained untended, mildewed scum forming in its corners. Her car ashtray overflowed with cigarette butts, some still lit and burning holes in the carpeted flooring where they had fallen. There were signs.

Either because Mother was *over* the adventure of the city or due to the cost of living and living alone, the summer after fourth grade we moved "home" to Texas, where she had grown up. Selecting a distance close enough for our connection to grandparents in Fort Worth but far enough away for her independence from her parents, she bought a traditional house in an upper-middle-class neighborhood in Houston and enrolled us in school.

Settling into our new world began happily. We were allowed to select paint, carpet, and even new furniture for our bedrooms. I went with robin's-egg blue paint; shag carpet stranded with blue, yellow, and green; and a modern and sleek walnut-stained bedroom set. With complementary paisley-patterned floor-to-ceiling drapes, my room became quite the showcase. It would eventually become my sanctuary.

It's around this time that my memories start to shift. Mother's juggling hands shake. The balls begin to fall to the ground. They are glass balls now, and I cut my feet on their shards.

....

EEEERRRRRRRRRRR! My days started with the sound of my mother's alarm down the hall. I pushed back the covers and padded into the kitchen, where I grabbed a glass, plunked in some ice cubes, and poured Coca-Cola over them. With a handful of chocolate chip cookies from the cookie jar, I made my way down the hall to my mother's bedroom. There I placed "breakfast" on her nightstand, turned off the alarm, and began the process of getting her up and ready for work. As a single mom, she needed to work, and it was my daily job to wake her up. Even though I was only about eleven, I could see it: my mother struggled with alcohol.

My mother was broken. I wondered what I'd done wrong and what I could do to fix her.

In my middle school years, I vacillated between good girl and not-so-good girl. Mine wasn't a long disobedience, but rather one where I carefully evaluated who I wanted to be and what road would take me there. I didn't know it at the time, but looking back now I can see that I, too, was broken. I stole cigarettes from my mom's skinny cigarette drawer and snuck down to the bayou in our neighborhood to smoke them. At one sleepover I sampled alcohol and ended up sick on bourbon and Coke. Eventually I looked at the other kids in my class, those experimenting with all things rebellious and those who weren't. There were "popular" kids in both sects. I decided to go the nonrebellious popular route and cut out most of the bad stuff.

Most of it. I still had my moments. Once I hurled raw eggs through my good friend's open front door on Halloween night, ruining her mom's wallpaper. At one of my mom's friend's weddings I downed eleven glasses of champagne—*eleven*—only to arrive home in my date's arms, launching my insides that were reminiscent of raw eggs. Ugh . . .

When I was sixteen I became a Christian—but I'd been becoming a Christian my whole life. Way back when I was a kid in California, my mom dropped my sister and me off at the neighborhood Presbyterian Church on Sunday mornings. We went to Sunday school and sang in the adult choir because we needed something to do to fill the time until she picked us up again. "Lo how a rose e're blooming." I had no idea what those words meant, but I sang them with feeling in my oversized burgundy choir robe and creamy satin stole. Once, walking down the long church hall toward a portrait plate collection of Jesus and the disciples hung on the wall, I felt an eerie-perfect draw of his eyes to mine. He was *real*.

In my teen years, when I heard that there was a specific process to becoming a Christian, I was dismayed that I'd been so slow to know and respond. My heart grieved that I'd somehow done even this—loving God—wrong, and I wrestled with whether he'd felt somehow slapped in the face by my ignorance. Blinded, praying for forgiveness, I plunged ahead and gave my life to Jesus. Maybe now I'd get it right? Maybe now life would heal up?

One night Mother and I argued over just how great a dad my dad was. (I think this was the season when I began to refer to my mother by her first name: Paige.) My position: he was not so great. Paige defended him: He provided. He cared. He just didn't show it. To her credit, she never said anything bad about him.

That very night I had a dream in which I saw myself falling off a high cliff, into what looked to be flesh-colored rocks far below. But as I landed, the rocks surprised me with their softness. They were not rocks after all, but rather the huge hands of God. I heard a voice saying, "I am your heavenly Father—I will never leave you nor forsake you."

I tucked these words away, wondering, *Could such a thing be true?*

I looked longingly at the seemingly perfect families of my friends. The fathers who predictably left for work in the morning and returned each evening. The moms who dressed in pretty outfits, sprayed their hair high, and wore lipstick, pearls, and pumps. The on-time family dinners around family tables in family homes. I wanted what they had. I determined that one day I would make a family immune from the brokenness and pain my first family had experienced.

It was a tough go, though. My mother continued to weave down the hall late at night, pinballing her way between the walls, glass of Scotch in hand. Smashed.

On one visit in my teen years I remember looking my father in the eye and asking if we could spend more time together. He raised one eyebrow and said, "As long as you are dependent on me for money I will never love you." *Crash.*

After college, a six-year relationship with my high school love ended—one that I'd assumed would culminate in marriage. Broken. Symbolically now a divorcée myself, I wincingly realized I shared this state with my mother. I hadn't thought such a thing would happen to me. I increased my determination to avoid creating a broken family—of any kind—myself.

In the aftermath of the breakup I struggled to figure out just what to do with the rest of my life. (I was at the tail end of twenty-one.) After all, for six years my life had been connected to a guy who planned to be a doctor, so I'd planned to be a doctor's wife. What training did that require?

A friend presented me with an embroidered plaque that read, "'For I know the plans I have for you,' declares the LORD, 'plans to prosper you and not to harm you, plans to give you a hope and a future'" (Jeremiah 29:11 NIV). I took the verse at face value. God knew: the plans—for me—for good—for hope and a future—for me.

Gradually I clarified God's call on my life and enrolled in

seminary, where I explored and confirmed God's call to ministry. I dated pretty much every unmarried student and then called a moratorium on men. Surprisingly, I then met and later married my husband. Precious, stable, rock of a man. We pledged to each other a no-matter-what kind of love. For keeps. Forever. Because Evan had incurred and survived cancer a few years prior, we knew we'd be unable to have children biologically and so immediately began the process of adoption. I continued my determination to make a *whole* family, one not marked by the pain and broken-ness I'd experienced, though postponing it for a while.

The *forever* process of adoption dragged on, and I cried out to God that I could hardly wait to give to my child what I'd never received: wholeness. I longed to love into their lack. To fill their void. In a hushed heart-whisper I heard God's gentle prodding, *Elisa, by the time you receive your child, he or she will have already experienced the greatest wound of his or her life.* I knew this was truth. It vibrated through my soul with reality. My baby would inevitably be wounded by the choice of his or her birth parents, even in a very loving decision to relinquish their baby. But I shushed the whisper and clung to the hope that I could create for another the family I'd never experienced myself.

Finally—after a long wait—our adoption came through, and I mothered first one and then another child. Motherhood! A baby! Love! At last! I lapped it up, licking around all the edges. We thrived in those early years of parenting and familyhood. Church was our second home. We had "Jesus time" every night. Great friends modeled mothering for me and fathering for Evan. Family dinners around a family table in a family home.

I happily hunkered down into those early mothering years, investing my skills and gifts in my kids—at *last*! But I struggled in some ways that surprised me.

One afternoon naptime revealed a reality of my mothering—of *me.* I loved that waking time of cuddles and kisses. But when I gathered my three-year-old daughter up in a hug, I discovered her pants were wet. Again. Like so many other mothering moments, I defined *my* success by *her* actions. I felt *I'd* never get this potty training thing down.

I sat her in front of the TV—*Sesame Street* in those days— balled up the wet sheets *again*, and made my way to the basement laundry room. There I stuffed them in the washer and then was stunned to watch above my head an arc of detergent whirling in the air. Coming straight from the box. Making a mess! The box was attached to an arm. I followed the arm down and discovered— amazingly—that the arm was mine! I was hurling detergent in my basement all the while yelling like an adult in a *Charlie Brown* cartoon! *Wa wa wa wa wah wah!* As I listened intently I translated: "Why do *I* have to be the one to have all the answers? To be in charge? Why can't *I* be the one to ask the questions?" I refer to this moment as my Suds Slinging Incident. Motherhood revealed me to myself. I was needy and broken. Such a thing surprised me, as I'd expected to be *better* at this. More confident. I knew God, after all.

A few years after this moment, my phone rang and a member of the board of MOPS International was on the phone asking me to consider applying to become the first president of this then fifteen-year-old grassroots movement for moms. What were they thinking? What was God doing? Me? The daughter of divorce and alcoholism? Sure, I'd been to seminary. Yes, I had been ID'd as a leader all my life, and I knew God had called me to ministry. But me and mothering? I laughed! So Sarah-like, when as an old woman she was told she'd have a baby. Ha!

Nevertheless, I agreed to pray about the request and doubled up on my therapy sessions. In line at the grocery store I looked around at the other mothers—in sweats, in work clothes, with their kids in various forms of obedience and disobedience—and I saw in their eyes the same Swiss cheese holes I had experienced in my soul. I felt God was saying to me, *Elisa, let your deficits be your offering.* Terrified, I accepted the invitation, applied, was offered the job, and then served as CEO of MOPS International for twenty years, touching over a million moms during those decades.

Even as president of an international organization for moms, there were other mothering moments that underlined my inadequacy, my Mother Inferior reality, my stature as Mother Elisa, not Mother Teresa.

Monster Mom made her appearances—once over cat vomit on the stair landing where I screamed, "Is the *mother* the only one in the house who knows what cat vomit looks like? Is the *mother* the only one in the house who knows where the paper towels are?" I slammed my way to the garage, where I crashed metal garbage can lids together in cymbaled rage, all the while hollering at the wide-eyed family members on the other side of the closed door, at the air, at God.

I wondered, *Would I be enough? As a mom? As a woman?* In my heart of hearts I wanted desperately to create an unbroken family. What if I couldn't? What if I actually contributed to further breakage?

....

During these decades Evan and I both invested our professional lives in nonprofit, cause-driven work. We continued loving and raising children who, we purposed, would one day be independent of our provision, would invest in our world in meaningful ways, and would live out their faith by loving and serving Jesus and his ways.

One night when my kids were in their teen years, I had a dream. I was walking with Jesus through a home under construction. Our home. I paused at a doorway to a bedroom—with another bedroom beside it. Jesus turned to me and said, "These rooms are for your daughter and her baby." I laughed and said, "She isn't pregnant. She's just a teenager!" To this Jesus responded, "Yes, she is."

When I awoke, I shook it off. But a few nights later the dream repeated itself. Even more concerning, a few days later as I sat in a meeting listening to research on teen moms with our team and considering the creation of Teen MOPS groups, I heard God heart-whisper again, *Elisa, you are going to know more about this subject than anyone around this table.*

I decided I should probably check in with my daughter. I asked, "Is there any possibility you could be pregnant?" My amazing daughter, just back from nurturing HIV/AIDS orphans in a Kenyan orphanage with her church youth group, my varsity swimmer medalist child, my full-of-life budding beauty, looked at me and nodded . . . *yes*. Stunned, I worked to take in her response. I—never-pregnant me—drove to the grocery store and purchased a pregnancy test. I took it home and stood outside the bathroom door while my child peed on a stick to reveal that, indeed, she was pregnant.

To me it seemed that my family fell and broke into a thousand pieces. Again. I wondered what I could do to fix my family now.

But it wasn't just my daughter who surprised me—and there are so many more layers to this story yet to be told. During those knock-me-off-my-feet years, my son began to leak out his pain. Perhaps because his sister's teen pregnancy became the screen on which he watched his own intrauterine development play out, as his birth mom was fifteen when she'd conceived and then relinquished him. Maybe his addictive genes were at work or maybe his own anger issues. Maybe it was my mothering deficiency (of course it was that, I concluded!). For whatever reason, my state-ranked swimmer, wry-witted delight, and tenderhearted son started down a slope of veering choices: pot, alcohol, truancy, troubled relationships, legal and money issues . . . losing himself.

The prospect of penning annual Christmas letters left my husband and me howling. Sure, with pain, but now also with black humor. We received stacks of end-of-the-year summaries from friends and acquaintances: "Rachel is an honor student at Stanford and headed to the mission field in Ecuador, and John Junior has signed a six-figure book deal, will be speaking nationally sharing his faith, and is bound for the Olympics. Hunter (the dog) just caught a mouse that has terrorized our home. We are so proud!"

In response we composed, "Our children are about to graduate! One from probation, the other into independent living. Our dog only threw up on the carpet four times this month!"

We never actually sent that letter, but oh, how inadequate we felt in comparison to the "perfect" families we read about. Today I hear from friends, and even my kids, how very much they wish we *had* sent our make-believe Christmas letter! Why do we do this to ourselves?

Here's the thing: I thought it was my fault that my first family broke, so I determined it was my responsibility to make an unbroken family in my second one. Problem is, I'm broken. Everybody is. So no matter what we do, we all end up making broken families. In one way or another.

Does this bump you? That everybody is broken and so everybody makes broken families? Is there a "But, but, but . . ." welling up in your throat? A "Hey, my family's not that bad!" kind of wail? Gentle now . . . but honest: there is no such thing as a perfect family. And as long as we push this truth into the closets and cubbies of our well-planned and perfectly decorated family homes, we'll be worshipping the false idol of the impossible. And likely missing some very rich realities in our very real lives.

I come from a broken family. And despite my very best attempts to produce a formulaically perfect Christian family in my second—the reality is that I *still* come from a broken family.

"'*For I know the plans I have for you,*' *declares the* Lord." Plans for me—for good—for hope and for the future. I look at those words today and have to admit, in so many moments God's plans haven't looked so good to me. But they have been. Good. Maybe just a different kind of good? (Besides . . . I'm sure those words from Jeremiah to the Israelites didn't always seem *good* to them either.)

Today I've been married nearly thirty-five years. (Yes, that dear, stable soul has stayed!) We have two adult children: a son and a daughter and grandson—and her husband—in that order. We are messy. We are imperfect. Gooey in the middle still. All of us. My husband and I express our love for Jesus in full-time ministry. We're involved in church. We pray over our meals. And we still slip into overresponsibility, we meddle in our kids' lives, at times we forget to surrender.

My grown kids are paving their own paths. They love Jesus. Sometimes they go to church. They pray in text messages. They evidence their beliefs in inked symbols on their bodies.

My daughter expresses her love for Jesus in listening to people's woes and wonders—with an exceptional emotional intelligence—while she cuts and styles their hair. She loves her son with fierceness and advocates for him at every turn. Her husband stands at her side through this-that-and-the-other medical issue and yields his heart toward good, even refusing to kill an intruding praying mantis but rather ushering it out of their house with a broom.

My son turns the pages of his Big Book, works the Twelve Steps, and bows his head with his sponsor. He's transitioning the evil markings on his arm into symbols of redemption. He hugs until the air leaves our lungs. He looks my husband in the eye and thanks him for yet another chance. He is falling in love with a wonderful woman. He turns his heart outward to offer grace to others.

We continue—each of us in unique and stumbling steps—the journey toward Jesus and Christlikeness. Instead of the dreamed-for final product of an unbroken family, I find my family and the people in it—myself included—still broken and in need of mending, and somehow likely looking more like we were meant to look all along.

I come from a broken family. I *still* come from a broken family. I'm pretty sure I'm not alone.

....

Lament *is a cry of belief in a good God, a God who has His ear to our hearts, a God who transfigures the ugly into beauty.*

—ANN VOSKAMP[1]

Right Where God Wants Me

It was a quiet Sunday afternoon. I'd returned a few hours earlier from a speaking engagement and then enjoyed the delight of putting my grandson, Marcus, down for his nap in our upstairs "Marcus" room while his mommy worked. Now I was resting. What an "old" word! But in that moment, it fit, and I gave in to it.

Until I heard an unrecognizable eruption. A crash? A long, loud falling and breaking sound. I couldn't imagine its cause.

Had it come from outside the house? Hugging myself, I began a search-and-rescue mission through the main floor of my home. Nothing out of order in the bedroom or bath. The family room and kitchen still stood where they should. The entryway? Fine. The living room? Okay. Ah . . . the dining room.

A realization from deep in my core trickled up to my mind, offering me enough clues that I had to admit the undesirable cause. I didn't have to enter the room to check my instinct. But I did. Once within, I took in what I'd dreaded to see. A three-shelf unit containing my grandmother's antique china collection had lost its grip on the wall and tumbled to the floor. The plates, all hand-painted, many of them portraits of eighteenth-century European royalty, and many signed by their artists, lay in shards beneath the unit.

I knelt and carefully lifted a corner of the shelving set. What lay beneath was dismal. Shattered treasures. For decades my grandmother, Munna, had acquired each plate as a memory of a trip she'd taken with other elderly women in tourist buses across Europe. I remembered her returning, carefully removing their bubble-wrap cocoons, and unraveling the stories of their painted scenes as she held them out before me. When she died, they were the one item I wanted to remember her by. A beautifully illustrated display of life lived out on porcelain plates.

As I gingerly lifted fragment after fragment the severity of the situation hit me. There was no remedy here. I located one single saucer with minor damage out of a set of twenty-some relics. The rest . . . well, clearly my inherited plate collection was beyond help.

The past few years had been tough. My daughter a single mom. My son struggling in the throes of adolescence and more. Heavy leadership responsibilities. So much of my life felt like the broken mess on my dining room floor. Beyond help.

A sharp realization sliced through my thinking. I pictured God— my gracious heavenly Father—tenderhearted and bending low. *Now you're talking,* he mused. Beyond help. It's just where he wants me.

Beyond my best efforts. Beyond my put-on-a-happy-face clichés. Beyond self-help methodologies. Beyond being better than anyone else. Beyond worrying about what doesn't matter anyway. Beyond everything being all up to me: to understand, to care, to give, and to fix.

That Sunday afternoon I stared at a stack of antique shards representing a heritage now rooted not on my wall but in my heart. Marcus's voice came to me from the baby monitor.

I looked at the mess on my floor. Broken. Beyond help.

Indeed, I was. Thank God.

2

Our Broken Families

The Sunday paper sits on the kitchen counter. Evan has laid it there while he makes coffee. I flip through the sections until my hands stop, paused by a headline: "Lesson Plan for an A+ Parent."[1] Great. More mythology.

What's an A+ Parent? Who creates a lesson plan to produce one? I used to think I knew exactly how to be an A+ Parent and that my efforts were *sure* to produce A+ Kids. I even taught workshops on the subject. But now—in my adult child and grandparenting era I was seriously reassessing. So much had changed in my world, in me.

My thoughts drift back to a morning just a few years back and how I began to embrace—and eventually enjoy—the new normal of my family life. Grandson Marcus and I piled into the car with his loot in tow. Homework paper? Check. Backpack? Check. Jacket? Check. Friday folder? Check. Overnight bag? Check.

He buckled himself into place behind me as I backed out of the garage. We sang "Noah's Ark" as we drove the four blocks up the street to his school, where I would drop him for the day before turning left out of my neighborhood and making my way fifteen more minutes to my office. As we pulled into the parking lot we punched the speed-dial on my phone, and Marcus's mom answered.

"Hey, Buddy! Have a great day! Did you have fun with Yia Yia and BeePeez?" (That's "Marcus-ese" for me and his grandfather.) My daughter thanked me for having Marcus overnight, and then we trundled on into his classroom, where he stashed his stuff in his cubby. Remembering that Marcus would be picked up by his birthfather after school, I rehearsed the routine to take his overnight bag and remember to do his weekend homework. With a knowing nod, this little five-year-old assured me he "had it" and turned, eager to join in circle time. I blew him a kiss and headed out.

A normal morning in the life of a normal preschooler. The normal backpack and homework. The normal songs and routines. The normal smooches and hugs. And what has become the new normal grandparent/mom/stepdad/birthparent/community family of the preschool-age child. I never saw it coming, but here it is—and I've been living it out full-time.

In the years prior to and since my new normal grandparenting, my broken family ushered me into season after season of surprising trauma. I've come to know that I'm not alone. At some point, we all find ourselves sweeping up fragments, whether of our own family efforts or with friends and extended family whose lives are somehow shattered.

What do your days look like? I hear from so many of you—your daily realities intersecting with mine.

Jessica calls me to tell me that when she's driving her fifteen-year-old Brianna to school one morning her daughter tells her that she hears people talking to her. People who aren't there. My mouth goes dry.

I work with Cyndi. One day she's called home from her office by the police. She arrives to discover her fourteen-year-old son dead from a self-inflicted gunshot wound. There are no words. Only wails and howls and bowed heads that can't find a way to look up.

Judy's son leaves home, and she has no idea where he's gone. She wonders where God's gone too: "Haven't we all been praying for this boy? Where is the change, the redemption, the restoration, the answered prayer?"

Richard is a Christian leader in my world. I respect him deeply and count on his wisdom. He confides that his daughter is having anxiety attacks. Big time. She's also pulling out her hair.

Bonnie writes me that her grown son and his girlfriend are moving in together. She confesses, "It feels like a loss (again) because as you raise your kids, and you feel you are doing the best job possible, they make choices that rob you of a piece of the dream. I'm so disappointed!"

Jen e-mails that her son is in jail and her teenage daughter is pregnant. She's a pastor's wife. She can't imagine telling anyone the news. She tells me.

Laura's son reveals that he's gay. She's always wondered, but she asks me on the phone, "Now what?" I picture her sweet face and her earnest, knitted brow. This is a mom who has spent years on her knees. Down she goes again.

It's not just the kids I hear about. John tells Rebecca he wants a divorce. Carol is diagnosed with ovarian cancer. Josh is laid off from work. Phil can't get his wife out of bed in the mornings.

These are real stories of real people I know and love. Really. I didn't even change most of the names.

Technically, a broken family is simply one where members of a family don't live together due to the effects of divorce or separation. Studies indicate that the potential negative effects of broken families result in "splintered" children, including poor performance in school, learning disabilities, child abuse, mental illness, and delinquency.[2]

But today's families are broken in far more ways than in just living arrangements. From diabolically complicated to everyday realities, broken families abound. The word *broken* means "shattered, crushed, sorrowful, bankrupt, disconnected."[3]As I look around from the vantage point of my own first and second broken families, I realize I'm surrounded by broken families. Broken in different ways and for different reasons.

Families are broken relationally. One-half of all American children will live in a single-parent home at some point in their lives. One-third are born to an unmarried parent (one-eighth to a teen mom). One-fourth live with only one parent and one out of twenty-five live with neither parent. Many in this last category live with a grandparent, while some are in foster care.

Seven out of ten children today live in what is defined as a nontraditional family—where a married man and woman do not head up the household. Of these "new normal" children, approximately 23 percent live full-time with their biological moms and 4 percent live with their biological dads. Thirty percent of these children live in stepfamilies.[4]

Like me and my original family. Like my grandchild's new normal family.

Families are broken financially. The average family has over $7,000 in credit card debt, and even if they pay the minimum monthly payment, it will take them decades to pay it off. The average mortgage debt is $149,000, and the average student loan debt is $34,000. The unemployment rate hovers around 8 percent.[5] Nobody has enough saved for retirement. Health insurance, college tuition—the list goes on. Just buying school supplies slays most parents.

I remember when my mother saved for a *year* to buy our family a color TV in the sixties. Today it takes one paycheck to buy a TV—and a *year* to save for insurance.

Families are broken spiritually. Americans are becoming less Christian. David Kinnaman of Barna Research reports:

- 25 percent of people over forty are not Christian
- 40 percent of those under forty are not Christian[6]

And the outlook for the future shows a continued decline. According to Kinnaman, "There is a 43 percent drop-off between the teen and early adult years in terms of church engagement. These numbers represent about eight million twentysomethings who were active churchgoers as teenagers but who will no longer be particularly engaged in a church by their thirtieth birthday."[7] These young men and women are the future moms and dads of the next generation.

A server at Chili's took the credit card of my lunch partner. It must have been from a Christian credit union, as it was illustrated with three crosses and John 14:6: "Jesus answered, 'I am the way, and the truth, and the life. The only way to the Father is through me.'" The server eyed it and responded, "Wow. This guy John sounds really conceited."

When my grandson, Marcus, shared in his Kindergarten Star of the Week program that his favorite book was his Jesus Book and his favorite story was David and Goliath, no one had ever heard the story before. One kid asked if that was a story in the book without the pictures.

Families are broken in their expectations. Perhaps this is the largest fissure of all in the fallen family. Bottom line, we *all* expect families to produce the impossible. We've come to believe that our families can define, rate, and actualize us as individuals. We parents are broken in our expectations as to what God really hopes we'll achieve in raising our children and in what is actually possible for families. Beneath our A+ lesson plans, we've come to believe that our families can actually save us.

We preach that if we are godly enough as parents, we will produce godly offspring. Family holidays, family rules and chores, and consistent, biblical family values yield perfect families. We chant, "Train children to live the right way, and when they are old, they will not stray from it" (Proverbs 22:6) like a spiritual magic spell, when that verse is anything but a formulaic promise. Rather, it is a premise—a wise principle—interpreted in myriad manners by the most brilliant theologians. (A: If you train up a child according to the bent of his or her personality, he or she will continue to grow in such a direction. B: If you build a spiritual foundation into a child as a young person, he or she will surely look back and consider such beliefs as he or she develops.)

Stunningly, we are humbled into place by the reality of DNA—heredity—and ... oops! ... sometimes our results don't yield the desired outcome of our actions. Addiction rears its head. A learning disability. Personality traits. Intelligence—or lack thereof. A disease. Recent research suggests that genetics may have a more powerful effect on how a child turns out than our own parenting practices.[8] Yikes! Where's God? Oh yes, he can intercede, right? But when he doesn't do what we pray, then what?

A noted seminary chancellor once told my husband, "A combination of three elements shape how our children turn out: environment, heredity, and personal choice." We can't control that last one at all.

There's no such thing as a perfect family.

Today's family is hungry for an honest and authentic assessment of what we can *really* expect to achieve as a gathering of people related by birth, adoption, marriage, and choice—a family. The era of the 1950s and then the cycle of the 1970s have passed. The days of triumphalism—trending always up and to the right—are over. Rebellion, addiction, illness, dysfunction, divorce, bankruptcy, and deep disappointment have debunked the formula for turning out an intact, perfect family. We sit among the shards of our shattered dreams and swat at guilt and grief, while fingering the memories of genuinely good times. And *still* we long for the intact. In the 2007 movie *Juno*, the raw tale of a teen mom who relinquishes her baby through adoption, the main character pledges, "I want things to be perfect. I don't want them to be broken . . . like everyone else's family."[9]

It's kinda scary to admit this, isn't it? That our families are broken? We run the other way from such a confession. No way will we let our family be lumped into the catchall phrase of shame: *broken*. As blogger Amy Martin suggests, the mantra of the church is *"Everyone is accepted as they are,"* but *"That person is not ok, we must fix them,"* is the practice.[10]

Sociologist Brene Brown's TED talk on vulnerability has garnered more than 7 million hits.[11] For good reason: we are hungry for the freedom to say what is so. She pushes us to embrace our own brokenness—with the reality that we are not alone in it:

> We are "those people." The truth is . . . we are the others.
>
> Most of us are one paycheck, one divorce, one drug-addicted kid, one mental health diagnosis, one serious illness, one sexual assault, one drinking binge, one night of unprotected sex, or one affair away from being "those people"—the ones we don't trust, the ones we pity, the ones we don't let our children play with, the ones bad things happen to, the ones we don't want living next door.[12]

The family is not a formulaic, perfectable institution where . . .

A (Active Family Meetings)
+ **B** (Bible Reading and Memorization)
+ **C** (Church Attendance)

PCFWAWANB (Perfect Christ-Followers Who Are Whole and Not Broken)

This is a *lie*—and I'm tired of it. Broken by it. It's a lie from which there is no healing, only shamed defeat.

Today I apply this raw reality of our universal brokenness—and my unique flawedness—in my world as I sit in the front row and prepare to speak to an audience. The speaker before me introduces her lovely woman-child who passionately offers her testimony and punctuates the climax with a song. In perfect pitch. I feel less-than.

The applause settles. I climb the steps to the platform and take my turn behind the pulpit, the voices in my head telling me I must *not* reveal the reality of my messiness. Instead, I must perpetuate the myth of perfect family values, dressing up in a disguise of Über Woman. It's what people *want*, isn't it?

I look into eyes. I sense the hunger. I feel the pain. No, such a pretense is what we *think* we want. What we've been programmed to expect. I inhale. I dig deep. I pray. And I give from who I am and what God has allowed and accomplished within me. God takes my words and sifts them to meet the needs present in those listening. I tell my story. I share God's presence in my journey. Yielded. Messy. Imperfect. Real. Broken.

Back in my seat on the front row I raise my gaze and hear the next speaker tell of God's provision through her pain. In conclusion, she introduces her adult son—still in progress but seemingly so much further along than my grown but gooey-in-the-middle children. Once again I wrestle the spears of inadequacy down to the ground and focus on the *good* in God's work. All of it in all of us.

Broken beings: this is who we are. Broken us. Every one of us. There is no one righteous. Even those who get up again—praise them and praise God!—have fallen at some point, thus necessitating the getting back up. When they are up, I slay my internal accusers and celebrate. "The Lord is close to the brokenhearted and saves those who are crushed in spirit" (Psalm 34:18 NIV).

These words are from King David—a follower after God's heart who fell and sinned and rose to try again. But they could just as easily be from me. Or the speaker before me. Or her daughter. Or the speaker after me. Or her son. Broken families are an equal-opportunity employer.

Can I just say this? Again?

There is no such thing as a perfect family.

Look around.

Everybody struggles with something, though at varying degrees of denial and admitting. While truth-telling this reality may end our fairy-tale expectations, it's not the end of the universe. In fact, admitting our brokenness may be the most freeing and beautiful release we ever experience.

....

Parenting, like all tasks under the sun, is intended as an endeavor of love, risk, perseverance, and above all, faith. It is faith rather than formula, grace rather than guarantees, steadfastness rather than success that bridges the gap between our own parenting efforts, and what, by God's grace, our children grow up to become.

—LESLIE LEYLAND FIELDS[13]

Church

I went to church last night. My husband and twentysomething son went as well. Evan and I parked the car and walked up the steps where we met Ethan, just finishing a cup of coffee. Together we entered a room of people, lined in chairs, facing the front, and a tidy African-American teacher named Jerry punctuating his points with fingers spread toward heaven. His neat gray beard provided scenery for his brilliant smile and captivating eyes. The subject was, for him, one of passion.

Chairs were scarce, but we found a stack of stored folding ones and carried them to the back, where we positioned them together, peeled away our coats, and seated ourselves with the other members. I looked around at them. A businessman cloaked in cashmere. Forty-ish folks in golf shirts and straight-from-work garb. A few young men with mud-caked boots. Older teens trying out new longer-look hair. Women of all ages in heels, in espadrilles, in boots, in running shoes. Occasionally Jerry invited participation, and here and there, he received honest, thoughtful responses.

When Jerry completed his talk, the room broke for coffee and whatnot and then reassembled in breakout rooms for smaller discussions. There, we celebrated the communion of lives. Sins were confessed—sometimes haltingly, and in other moments freely. In every case, eyes met eyes and both the wounded and the victor were received.

Our family's turn came. Ethan started and said he'd had a pretty good week, that he'd been journaling, that he was working out things with his boss, and that he felt he was just breaking the ice on so many issues. I went next and talked about risking trust in broken places.

Evan opened up and processed his desire to "fix it" in the family. Our comments were met with nods and a hushed, sacred understanding.

Once all had taken their turn, the ceremony was completed. We stood, embraced, bowed our heads, and prayed. On leaving, my heart was lighter. My bonds with my family were stronger. My experience of God's presence was closer. And my belongingness to a body of broken believers was more intense.

I went to church last night, and there I discovered a body of God's pilgrims, finding their way one day at a time on the journey of recovery. Oh, God, that the established church of our world could look a bit more like a gathering of AA. Then maybe more of us would want to go more often and be more real there and in our world.

3

God's Broken Family

It's tempting to freak out over the fact that our families are broken—to think that if we fix the issues of marriage, money, and faith, we'll fix the future of our families, and *voila!*—all will be well. But in reality, broken families are not new. We *all* come from a broken family because God's family is broken. The thing is, this isn't the tragedy we assume. Broken is right where God wants us—and right where he can powerfully reassemble us.

In the beginning, God created man and woman. Adam and Eve were a family, a man and a woman evidencing the image of God in their beings and in their union. But before they even got around to making children, they fell and broke. The original family was a broken family—separated from the very heart of God. The very first child was born into this broken, messy family.

In the space of the first five chapters of the Bible, man and woman became one, disobeyed God's only prohibition, and gave birth to two sons, one of whom murdered the other. The result is that by Genesis 6, the inhabitants of the planet were those whose hearts were turned so wholly toward evil that God decided to start over again.

God's heart broke over his broken family.

The second time around, the results were no better. God started again with one family—this time Noah's. For forty days and forty nights they did okay together. But once the Flood ended, Noah and his sons lost their footing—and the downfall of the family continued.

- At the request of his wife, who was impatient for a child, Father Abraham took their slave, Hagar, as his mistress and had an illegitimate heir.
- Jacob married one sister but actually loved—and *also* married—another.
- David committed adultery with Bathsheba and then murdered her husband.
- The prophet Hosea was betrayed by his unfaithful wife, Gomer, yet took her back.

In Scripture we find families built with love and chastity and families formed from rape and sin. Children born from one father to mothers who were sisters. Children born out of adultery, through prostitution, and into polygamous marriages. Children born to people of humble means and then relinquished through adoption to rulers and royals. And because respect didn't come naturally to his people, God had to *tell* them to honor their parents.

That's just in the Old Testament. The New Testament begins with an unwed—though betrothed—pregnant teenager . . .

....

We all come from a broken family and then create another broken family, because all families are broken. Even God's. In our brokenness, we are just where we need to be. Fractured. Messed up. Sinful. Needy. Redeemable.

Barbara Brown Taylor writes, "Pain makes theologians of us all . . . Pain is one of the fastest routes to a no-frills encounter with the Holy."[1]

There is beauty in the broken.

Our Creator God pants to bring his children into being, and then his heart tears in pain as we run, hide, and reject his love. Our Father God christens us sons and daughters and then releases us to our own stubborn ways but stands in the road, watching and waiting for us to return to him. Our hereafter God dreams of redemption, when we are restored to his original purposes and put in pleasant places in relationship to him and to each other.

Humankind is a broken, messy family. And we all come from this broken family. The family broke before it was even completely made. Just as *my* efforts fell short of fixing the breakage of my first and second families, *our* efforts will also miss the mark in making families whole and healthy in our broken world.

Think of it this way: If God's family was and is broken, why do we think ours will be any different?

Isaiah 53 prophesies that healing for the broken will arrive through an unexpected channel: a broken Messiah. In 53:2, the coming king is seen as less than lovely. Seemingly no "beauty in the broken" there. "He had no special beauty or form to make us notice him; there was nothing in his appearance to make us desire him." My pastor, Robert Gelinas, compared the beauty of Jesus to that of Fiona in *Shrek*. There was beauty in the princess, but it wasn't revealed until she became an ogre, revealing to Shrek and others her beauty from within.[2]

The beautification of brokenness appears as God's despised man of sorrows takes our infirmities upon himself. Isaiah 53:5 underlines God's provision for the broken heart, the broken soul, the broken human, and yes, the broken family. "But he was wounded for the wrong we did; he was crushed for the evil we did. The punishment, which made us well, was given to him, and we are healed because of his wounds."

The word "wounded" in this verse actually refers to bruises—black and blue marks created by broken blood vessels.[3] And the word "healed" comes from a root meaning "mended, repaired, thoroughly made whole—spiritually forgiven."[4] By his broken blood vessels that resulted in black and blue blotches we are made thoroughly whole.

Somewhere along my journey from my first broken family to my second broken family, I began to understand that the brokenness in my first family wasn't my fault. God led me through the layers of shame and fear to convince me: I had no control over my parents' choices. I didn't run my father off. I didn't force my mother to overdrink. Gently, God led me to the words of 1 John 4:18: "Where God's love is, there is no fear, because God's perfect love drives out fear. It is punishment that makes a person fear, so love is not made perfect in the person who fears." I realized that I did not need to fear because Jesus had already endured any punishment I might face. *We are healed because of his wounds.*

Hear me well: the brokenness inflicted on you in your first family is not your fault.

The years passed and I mothered my second family. In spite of my imperfect, broken places, gradually I faced the reality that God did not evaluate my mothering by how perfectly or imperfectly my children developed. Rather, he expected me to address how *I* influenced my children by how *I* yielded to his love for *me* and then acted it out in life. Period. He did not ask me to control *their* responses, *their* choices, or *their* consequences. I could throw my body over the potholes in their path, and they might or might not heed my warnings. I could not fix my family—my first family or my second—any more than I could fix myself. I was broken. They were broken. I was to offer myself to God and to allow him to use my best, but still flawed, mothering to shape their development. *By his wounds we are healed.*

While the brokenness you experienced in your first family is not your fault—remember that—there may be elements of brokenness in your first or second family that you are responsible for. If so, say so. It is up to you to take responsibility to right the wrongs and move toward healing. I've had to go to each of my children and my husband and confess my overparenting, my fear, my judgment, my inadequacy. At times the list of my failings has been so long that there was no gathering it up in my arms. I dragged it about behind me like a length of toilet paper stuck to my shoe. Humiliating, but necessary to notice and shake away.

Jesus alone has the power to heal the broken. Jesus alone has the power to save the lost. It's by *his* wounds that *we* find healing. Broken families find healing as the broken people within them admit their brokenness and yield personally to God's healing power. Rather than praying, "Make my family whole," we pray, "Make *me* whole."

When we are broken, we are exactly where God wants us. "Blessed are the poor in spirit, for theirs is the kingdom of heaven" (Matthew 5:3 NIV). When we are broken we are bankrupt. When we are bankrupt we are dependent. When we are dependent we are done with ourselves and open to God.

Crazy thing here: we tend to view our fallings as grounds for disqualification from meaningful ministry, from lasting relationships, from worthy contributions to our world—when exactly the opposite is true. When we fall and then turn to God for the hope and help he alone offers us, we can actually become *more* qualified for fuller living. Our brokenness makes us *more* able to invest in the lives of those around us as we bring God's healing of us to our relating to them.

Make your way through the pages of Scripture and you'll see human after human used more mightily after a fall than before. Abraham. Moses. Rahab. David. Ruth. Jonah. Peter. Mark. Paul.

Watch how God responds to the broken in Scripture.

God hallows broken people. "The sacrifice God wants is a broken spirit. God, you will not reject a heart that is broken and sorry for sin" (Psalm 51:17). When I admit I'm broken, I please God. To God, the broken are holy. Do you need to embrace this?

God holds broken people. "The Lord is close to the brokenhearted, and he saves those whose spirits have been crushed" (Psalm 34:18). Broken hearts are the terrain where God sows his perspective and waters it with his presence. When I reveal my broken heart to God, he comes near. God longs to gather the broken into his arms. Do you need to be gathered up by him?

God helps broken people. "He has sent me to comfort those whose hearts are broken" (Isaiah 61:1). When I expose my pain to God, he helps me navigate my way through it. God offers practical and spiritual help to the broken. He doesn't intend for us to remain in our pile of messed-up fragments forever. Do you need his help?

God heals broken people. "He heals the brokenhearted and bandages their wounds" (Psalm 147:3). When I offer my wounds to God, he heals them. God restores the broken to his desired purposes, then to dreams he possessed for us before time began. Do you need to be healed?

There's no such thing as a perfect family. Yet hope emerges through understanding that the broken family is anything but an unredeemable reality. Compassion comes as we understand that all of us—*every one of us*—is birthed forth from God's broken family. As we embrace our own need for mercy, we can extend grace to others. While vibrant and full of life, the healthy family of today is also gritty and real, a place where assembly and even reassembly is required. When we are broken, we are right where we need to be before God. And where we need to stay.

There is beauty in the broken.

It's time to leave behind the perfect family value mythology. In part 2, "Broken Family Values," I use my story to share values that God can use to build lasting families despite our brokenness. I pray you will discover first, that you are not alone; second, encouragement and perspective for your own journey; and third—most of all—that God bends to be with you in your brokenness.

Whatever kind of first family you come from and whatever kind of second family you make, you come from a broken family because God's family is broken. Gradually, with squinty eyes and yielded hearts, we can learn to see the beauty of broken and offer God's gift of brokenness back to him for his purposes in our world.

....

To be alive is to be broken; to be broken is to stand in need of grace.

—BRENNAN MANNING[5]

Telling Stories

I once read an interview in *Time* magazine with a celebrity—I've since forgotten which one—who said, "Every time you tell your story you give away a little piece of yourself." Telling our stories to others is expensive. It costs us—sometimes more than we care to spend.

Maybe that's why we can tend to s-t-r-e-t-c-h the truth now and then when we trot out our life experiences before an audience even of one or two. We aim to reduce the expense of sharing by "telling stories."

Over dinner, my husband asks about my day and, intent on winning the "I've had it worse than you" game, I launch into a tirade about handling a *million* phone calls and *seventy-six* projects and how *exhausted* I am. Sitting before an interviewer who queries me about my weaknesses, I sort through the reams of examples and settle on one that is least revealing. "I'm a perfectionist. I tend to work too hard."

Rearrangement of facts. Exaggerations. Partial truths. White lies. Putting ourselves in a good light. Blatant untruths. Hiding. There's a buffet of techniques at our fingertips to position ourselves as the heroines in our own stories, when in so many cases, we are both the tragic victims and occasionally the plundering villains.

Okay. Most of us rarely resort to outright lying. We know better. But every now and then—ooooh, the temptation to twist my facts. To s-t-r-e-t-c-h them. To edit. To make things—me—look better. Just a bit. What's with this?

Sometimes I stretch it *up*. I don't want to tell the *real* story because I fear losing power—and position. Once "out there," my story is open for others to interpret, to evaluate, to legitimize, or to judge. I don't like that. I want to be liked. What will others think of me if they know I struggle? Let me dress this up a bit. Package it with a principle: "God uses our messes." Maybe I could "grow into" this version of my story?

In other moments, I stretch it *down*. I'm not ready to face whatever lessons the story might teach. So I tell a simpler tale. One that won't raise eyebrows or elicit follow-up questions. Like many adult children, mine could use some financial help. I'm gooey in the middle on what's "right" in these situations. When asked about how we respond to their need, I avoid the topic with a comment about their jobs. I'm not exactly lying. I'm just not telling the hard truth.

Then there are the occasions where I stretch it *out*. My own story seems majorly messy to me. I don't want it to *be* my story, much less allow anyone else to *know* it's my story. So I tell a story that sounds like it's someone else's story when it's really mine. "Yeah, a friend of mine comes from a family of addicts and wonders if her overworking could be an addiction in disguise." The reason I know the story so well is because I lived it. I just don't want anyone to know it.

I think back to the celebrity's comment. Yes, telling our stories costs us. "Weren't you with Jesus of Galilee?" the servant girl asked Peter in the courtyard. "No. I don't even know him," he replied (Matthew 26:69–70). In the moment, Peter didn't want his story to be his story. He could have been led off to a cross there and then, just like Jesus. Later, after Jesus' death and resurrection, we find Peter not only owning his intimacy with Christ, but embracing the cost of expression as he tells his story before the Sanhedrin—in an equally expensive moment.

Every time we tell our story, we are giving away a little piece of ourselves. But that becomes a sacred offering. When we believe that God inhabits our lives in order to write in us an illustration of his love to us, then the telling of our story—*sans* s-t-r-e-t-c-h-i-n-g—will give a little piece of him away as well.

Part Two

BROKEN FAMILY VALUES

Anyone God uses significantly is always deeply wounded.... On the last day, Jesus will look us over not for medals, diplomas, or honors, but for scars.

—Brennan Manning[1]

4

Commitment

It had been a long day—the kind where everything came undone as soon as I did it. Preschooler insanity. I wiped bottoms and mouths and countertops, though not in that order, of course.

At last: bedtime. Evan was at a meeting, and I made it through the sweet night-night routine with Ethan, still a baby, and then three-year-old Eva, offering what I thought was pretty much mothering perfection. I'd embraced the myth of perfect parenting, fully expecting to create in my home what would become a perfect Christian family. Until, tiptoeing down the hall to my room for mommy time with a bowl of popcorn and the TV remote, I heard a toddler cry, "Mommy!" When I returned in a huff, my daughter wanted another drink, another book, another kiss—*more* of me. I didn't have more. I was on Empty. While I gritted my teeth and endured the moment, I knew I was a nasty fake. I reeked of impatience and anger. Where did such anger come from? By the time I turned out her light again and made it back to my room, I knew I didn't deserve mommy time. I thought, *I'm a lousy mother. The worst mother on the planet. I will ruin my children, I know it!*

Hannah's prayer from 1 Samuel 1:27–28 filtered through my mind: "I prayed for this child, and the Lord answered my prayer and gave him (her) to me. Now I give him (her) back to the Lord. He (she) will belong to the Lord all his (her) life." The words were embroidered on a pillow in my daughter's room. I'd expected to pray this prayer when Eva went off to college or walked down the aisle to be married—not when she was three. But mercy! I needed God to take over *now*!

God was listening. In fact, he piped right in, whispering to my heart, *Okay, Elisa, I'll take care of Eva. No worries. But do you trust me with her?*

"You bet!" I shot. "You are God!"

Do you trust me to walk her through a life-threatening illness?

"Err . . . yeah . . ."

Do you trust me to decide who she should marry, or if she doesn't marry, to provide for her?

"Well, I'd love a say in 'who'—but okay . . ."

Do you trust me to determine if she should go to public school or private school or be homeschooled?

"Can we just pick from option #1 or #2 here?" I pled. (Yikes!) And then, "Yes, I trust you with Eva."

Then, Elisa, do you trust me to choose for Eva the very best mother for who I know she will become?

I sat with that question a long time. Did I believe that God would pair me with my child—to be the mother she uniquely needs today and in the years to come? Was I up to the year-after-year-after-year commitment of knowing this truth and living it out in my actions? I still trace my finger along the edges of this truth today.

....

We had waited nearly five years for the call that our baby was actually *ours*. In the first stages of waiting, I was nonchalant about mothering. It would happen when it happened. Besides, I had more than a few questions about my fit for this role. Would I be a good mom? Would I know what to do? Would I love a baby the way other moms love their babies? My upbringing with my own mom was so ... unpredictable.

Yet the longer the wait stretched, the more I recognized an undeniable urge within me—an unfulfilled desire that would not be silenced. *I wanted a baby*. The process of adoption is like being in labor and dilated to an eight or nine for, like, *forever*. Everyone around us had kids. Baby showers tortured my soul. Mother's Day slashed my heart in shreds.

Finally, the call came on an Easter weekend. We would receive a three-week-old baby girl the next Monday. With hands held, Evan and I stood in church and soaked in the cross, decorated in Easter-lilied glory, while singing, "Christ the Lord is risen today—Alleluia!"

As we entered the agency's office the next morning, we heard the insistent cries of a baby. I rounded the corner of the waiting room to take in a tiny pink bundle wriggling on a cold, bare conference table while office workers chatted above her little body.

Someone pick up that baby! A primal drive released within me. An urge to respond. A call to act.

You're the mother, Elisa.

And I was. I moved with certainty, picked up my daughter, and became her mother.

In those early years people said some strange stuff to me about mothering. At least stuff I thought was strange. The main message was this: "You are so selfless to adopt." Or, "You are making such a difference in your children's lives. They are so lucky to have you." Huh? The words felt clunky and mismatched to me. The only reason Evan and I adopted is that we wanted children and we couldn't have them biologically. We weren't self-less. We were self*ish*. I wanted a baby. I wanted to love a little one with the love I hadn't received from my own parents. I wanted to complete another being with my being.

A friend wooed me to embrace the mystery of motherhood, saying, "It's so amazing to look into your baby's eyes and see yourself mirrored back from their little soul. They are such a part of you."

I looked. Deeply. Nuh-uh. I didn't see *me* mirrored back from my baby's being. Instead I saw Eva. Precious, lovely, amazing for sure. But not bone of my bone or flesh of my flesh. Not *me*.

Someone gave me a poem about how adopted babies don't grow under our hearts, but in them. Yeah. But still, she wasn't *me*. She was *her*. I felt a responsibility to know *her*, not the *me* I was told to look for in her. The words God had heart-whispered months before echoed back to me: *By the time you hold your baby in your arms he or she will have already experienced the greatest wound of his or her life.* I looked into her eyes and wondered.

Judge Brian Boatright, appointee to the Colorado Supreme Court and adoptive father, expressed, "Adoption is a promise acted out over a lifetime."[1] That was more like it.

In those early years I stayed home with my kids pretty much full-time. God tapped me for certain beyond-the-home efforts: a radio program for the college and then for the seminary, a neighborhood Bible study. I began to write articles and then a book—ironically: *I'm Tired of Waiting!* Our second child, Ethan, came, and I poured myself into adoring him, amazed at the effortless stretch in my heart to love him just as much as I loved his sister.

When my kids were five and three, the phone rang with the

surprising invitation to apply to become the first president of MOPS International. Inadequacy accused me at every angle. But Evan and I prayed and processed, and eventually I plunged into a world where God transformed my very deficits into my offering.

A menagerie of friends and sitters covered the hours Evan and I were away from our kids. Our family thrived. Eva—her name means "full of life"—burst into friendships and hobbies and the very joy of living. She struggled a bit in school but more than compensated with her natural ability to read and relate to people, both old and young. She came to know and love Jesus early on and grew in her love for him in Sunday school and VBS, and even took the top leader spot in her Christian summer sports camp. At least twice a year, she accompanied me on speaking trips, where we enjoyed special mother/daughter memories. And of course there were the normal Christmases, vacations, and everyday life where our family grew into its name. Along with her younger brother, Eva discovered swimming, and we invested hours and hours in carpooling and pooling, cheering them until they both achieved state rankings and Junior Olympian status. Eva was named to the varsity swim team as a sophomore and made the state high school team.

But in her heart, Eva struggled with a not-enoughness, a misfit kind of experience. "When will I fit in? When will the guys notice me?" she often asked on the way to school. Her pain made no sense to me. While I understood normal adolescent angst, I looked at my gorgeous, early maturing, full-of-life daughter and saw only beauty.

I still do. She is so very beautiful.

....

In her sophomore year, returning from a missions trip serving HIV/AIDS orphans, Eva forayed into new territory. For several weeks I watched her behavior shift ever so subtly. Moms' antennae catch such things.

That fall as I flew off to lead MOPS leaders and speak at our convention, most of my heart stayed behind with my daughter. Not yet knowing why, I struggled with a feeling that I needed to help her in some yet-undefined way. I watched God provide surrogates of support for her in my absence, but the tug at my heart continued. That year our theme at MOPS was "Sail on Through the Seasons of Life," focusing on Mark 6, where Jesus walks on the water to Peter. I was speaking on our need to get out of the boat to meet Jesus wherever he was—on the waves in our lives.

The night before I was to leave home, I had rotisseried in my covers, searching for sleep. I was tortured by the feeling I was going in the exact opposite direction I should be going: away from mothering. And I pictured myself out of the boat, on the waves, searching for Jesus. He was nowhere. Instead, I saw myself clinging to the side of the boat in a raging storm—and far across the waves, bobbing in the night, I saw Eva.

Then the next night, far away from home in my hotel room, the image returned. I wept as I saw my daughter, alone on the waves. In my heart God said to me, *Elisa, remember, Eva's a great swimmer.*

Someone wrote me a note: "Being a leader doesn't mean you have to leave your children all the time. But God is never more present to our children than when we are not."

In the weeks after I returned from that trip, the dreams and the heart-whispers from God led me to approach my daughter about her life. The discovery that our teenage daughter was pregnant rattled our world off its neatly swinging hinges. I admit, I actually ramped up my fix-it efforts in that season, negotiating her high school continuation with her teachers and swim coach, helping her hide her budding body beneath blousy fabrics, quietly connecting her with a teen pregnancy center so she could process her decisions for the future. I remember one day while I was at Target, shopping for maternity clothes with Eva, a neighbor stopped to chat and I actually positioned my petite frame in front of her tummy as if I could shield the sight of her protruding baby belly. I wanted to keep anyone from knowing. Why couldn't she have cancer? Then we could tell people. And they'd be sympathetic. They'd gather 'round and pray and ring our doorbell with casseroles. And it wouldn't be my fault.

At MOPS, I revealed our reality to the board and my team of senior leaders. Evan and I knew we needed the prayers and accountability of those to whom I reported and those with whom I worked. But we did not tell the rest of the staff, much less the constituency of moms I led. We didn't know what Eva would decide to do about the baby. We didn't know what we would decide to do to support her.

Early in her pregnancy—in fact, the night my daughter peed on the stick to find a plus sign appear—I asked her what she would do. She responded immediately, "Well, I'm not going to have an abortion." My throat clutched at her words. Of course she wouldn't, I agreed. But can I be honest? There was a moment when I wished that option *was* open in her heart. I looked at her life—and mine and the life of our family—as *forever* broken. Oh, would that there was a way *out* of this unexpected expectancy! A way where no one would have to know about it! Some path where we could just sweep over the footprints and make them vanish, as if she'd never set her foot down it. It was just a moment—but the thought rose real within me.

Another question filtered through my heart. Had I let her birthmother down? Ours was a closed adoption—in those days almost all adoptions were—so I didn't know her. But I was pierced with concern—no, guilt. After all, as a pregnant teen herself, she'd relinquished Eva to *my* care and now . . . well, surely she'd expected me to do more to avoid such a result.

As the baby grew within her, Eva wrestled with the choices open to her: keep the baby or relinquish the baby through adoption. Evan and I pried our hearts open to the reality that the decision was hers, not ours, while wrestling with the terror of just how she would survive either option. A baby? In our home? Wouldn't *we* become the parents? How would she make it financially? Without even a high school education? What would this mean for our ministries, for our lives? What would this mean for her future?

Note: I haven't mentioned the father of this pregnancy. That's because he was no longer part of Eva's life. He'd passed through over the summer and then vanished. We didn't know his whereabouts.

And I haven't mentioned yet much about Eva's brother, Ethan, and how her pregnancy affected him. That will come in other chapters.

Eva began to lean toward parenting. Around our kitchen table, with high school correspondence homework pushed to the side, we did the math and discovered that she and the baby would have to live with us for eight years before she'd be able to afford the very basics for them alone. It was a sobering moment. We punched the calculator off, rose from the table, and went about our individual lives, though such a thing barely existed as we were so increasingly interwoven.

I open my journal from these fork-in-the-road days and read a letter written but never given to my daughter:

> I long for you to have the freedom to grow into you. You are sixteen—so much in the process of becoming. While I know you can still find "you" while mothering, I also know that mothering takes up space and attention from that journey to becoming. A baby deserves the attention of its mother. But you deserve time and space to grow into "you" so that one day there will be enough of "you" to share with a child.

A few days later Eva told us she'd decided to relinquish her baby through adoption. She'd faced the reality of her dependency on us in order to mother, and she'd decided adoption would be best for her child. One question plagued her, though. "Am I being selfish?" I sat in awe at her maturity. Selfish? No, in my mind I knew she was taking yet another mothering step: selflessly choosing what was best for her child even if it ripped love from her own heart.

....

The next few weeks packed together meetings with the adoption agency and doctor visits. One afternoon Eva came home with the profiles of interested families. The process had begun. The wheels were in action. It seemed right, and a kind of peace settled in.

I found a card on my pillow. From the distinctive printed *Mom*, I knew it was from Eva. I tore open the envelope to find a snowy scene with a baby penguin front and center on the card within. I read:

Mom,
    You have meant so much to me my whole life but *really* right now. I don't know where I would be without you. You are like my best friend that I finally have the eyes to see. I thank you for listening to me and giving me the strength and the courage to push on . . . I'm so sorry that I'm putting you through all this. I wish that I could take it all back. I never mean to hurt you. I hope that you know that. I was thinking of a verse and can't think of all that it says but it starts with something like "If you put your trust in God, he will reward you . . ." I know that he is carrying you and showering all his blessings down on you.
                        Love you lots,
                        Eva

It carried me ahead.

Very early one morning, I awoke to find Eva standing by my bed. She'd started bleeding. She was twenty-seven weeks along. A long way still to go. We called the doctor, who instructed us to meet him in his office later that morning. There we learned that while he saw a small problem—a tear?—in the placenta wall, all was well, and he sent her home. The next morning at six she was bleeding again—a lot. We called again and were rushed to the emergency room, where she bled and bled and bled. When the doctor arrived, my sixteen-year-old daughter was in excruciating pain. After examining her, he used words I didn't understand: *placental abruption.*

Neither of us really knew what was happening. The labor and delivery classes were to begin the next week. I was to be Eva's birth coach. But we never got that far. Never-pregnant me—oh, how I wish I had been so that I might have better understood what was happening to my daughter! And novice Eva. Evan was ignorant as well. What a mess we all were! How unprepared.

The next hours blurred by—epidural, relief—sudden movement to the operating room where, swathed in yellow paper scrubs, I sat at her head while the doctor sliced through my daughter's abdomen and pulled a tiny baby boy from her womb. Two pounds something ounces. He was whisked away to emergency care while Eva cried and clutched her own baby blanket under the sheets. I hesitated, not sure just where to turn my care. Evan and I divided our focus. He picked up the primary caregiving role for the baby, while I stayed with our daughter.

In recovery, a kind nurse wheeled the baby toward Eva so that she could see him before he was airlifted in his incubator to another hospital with a better neonatal intensive care unit (NICU). He was beautiful. My daughter's long finger reached through the opening and touched her son's tiny face, and then he was gone. Evan followed the baby from one hospital to the next while I walked alongside Eva's hospital bed as she was taken to her room—alone.

The next few hours were surreal. Evan remembers the utter sacredness of his presence with the baby. As this new grandfather bent his head over the incubator, he prayed for the future of this little bundle. Wires and tubes and medical realities made it impossible for Evan to offer the comfort he longed to give. Yet just as he felt so helpless and questioned if this baby was wondering just where everyone had gone, Evan reached his finger through the opening in the cylinder and instantly, a finger no bigger than a strand of pasta grabbed on in response. There God was providing for us: Evan, me, Eva, the baby. Even there.

But our hearts tightened. What would happen next? How would God provide in the days to come? At twenty-seven weeks, his prognosis included cerebral palsy, brain damage, lung problems, and a host of other issues. Understandably, his needs were beyond the provision some adoptive parents might feel able to offer.

So Eva parented and Evan and I grandparented this precious baby boy, driving between office and home and NICU and praying like crazy for God to call forward a family to adopt him. Eva named him Thomas. It was a sweet name and served him well. God led us to a verse from Psalm 71:6: "From birth I have relied on you; you brought me forth from my mother's womb. I will ever praise you" (NIV). We wrote it on a card and taped it to his incubator.

At this stage I knew we couldn't hide our reality, and with the board's guidance, I told the entire MOPS staff of our ordeal. After the meeting a line grew to speak with me, and three separate individuals revealed they regretted having an abortion in their youth and how much they respected Eva's journey—and mine. Cards filled my mailbox with sentiments of support:

- "My heart goes out to you, mom to mom. I'm praying and so glad for who God is in your family."
- "Thank you for sharing your story. It is now my privilege to walk with you on this journey. I'm profoundly moved to know that you have endured such pain this year—and the shattering of your dreams."
- "May this be a time when you can receive from God and from the body around you—receive love, acceptance, grace, hope, and peace for you and your family."

....

Thomas arrives in March—over three months before his due date. No one is ready, including his own little body. He comes into a world that welcomes him, but the i's are not yet dotted, the t's not quite crossed. He sleeps in a bubble, tubes and needles and straps holding his purple limbs in place. They are threadlike small. Those limbs.

We three visit, taking turns sitting in a chair next to his life-giving cylinder, and poke our fingers through the handholes to gain access to him. The skin of preemies is so sensitive that to stroke it is to bring pain rather than the comfort we long to offer. Days later we are permitted to hold him without touching him on a pillow, for a bit at a time. Does he know us? Does he recognize our voices? Does he wonder why we come and go and who will eventually stay?

We call the adoption agency. Things are so unclear. Of course, we reconsider. Did we make the right decision? Is this turn of events a doorway offering us another chance to permanently parent and grandparent? But somehow his fragility reveals our own, and instead of changing her mind, Eva is more sure while also more broken. The sobering reality of knowing what she doesn't know, of not having what he needs.

Thomas not only survives day after day but begins to thrive. Now he is gaining weight, with no sign of any of the dreaded complications. But where are his parents? What is God doing?

One day the social worker calls. Do we know so-and-so? They have contacted the agency. They are asking if there's a Baby Morgan waiting for adoption. Yes, we know them, though not well enough that they might have called us directly. The couple had actually known Eva in her middle school days. We give permission for them to visit Thomas in the NICU, and they come. The story unfolds.

This woman, I'll call her Amanda, began to yearn for another child. She and her husband already had two children, but they felt God leading them toward another. Because this mom had a background in special education, she had no fear of any prognosis that might arise. They'd begun to pursue an international adoption—from Romania, perhaps? Her other children had been praying, nightly, for God to bring a new brother or sister into their family. One night Amanda was up late on her e-mail and received a message to pray for a baby in the NICU, for his healing, and that God would raise up a family to adopt him. Amanda sensed a fire shooting through her body—oh, how she *knew* this baby was to be *theirs*!—and woke her husband.

As Amanda followed up with the writer of the e-mail, she discovered that this baby, so full of desperate needs, had been born to Eva. The adoption agency set up visits with Thomas, and she and her family continued the discernment process. Was this child to be theirs? Were they called to be his parents? Amanda had known immediately—*yes*! But her husband hesitated. And then on Easter Sunday, God brought him clarity. They knew that God was *calling* them to permanently parent Thomas.

This is how Thomas came to belong to new parents—later than we wanted, but in perfect timing for his little life. We discovered their passionate waiting for Thomas was much like ours had been for our children. Longing. Waiting. Trusting God to match child with parent, and parent with child. In July our families joined in a conference room in the hospital where the social worker led us through a relinquishment ceremony and Eva gave "birth" to Thomas all over again, releasing him from her arms to the arms of his new family. "From birth I have relied on you; you brought me forth from my mother's womb. I will ever praise you." The card went home with him.

Thomas was completely provided for. As was Eva. And Evan and me.

Today we see Thomas now and then. It's an open adoption where we have access to each other. He is happy in his home. And he is free of cerebral palsy, brain damage, and the host of other complications he was predicted to carry. I will always love him from afar. We all will.

Decades ago in an agency office, I picked up a baby off a table and she became my daughter. In a moment when I felt not enough to be my three-year-old daughter's mother, I offered her to God. "I prayed for this child, and the Lord has granted me what I asked of him. So now I give her to the Lord. For her whole life she will be given over to the Lord." God's response? *Do you trust me to choose for Eva the very best mother for who I know she will become?* I had to learn to.

Commitment is love *no matter what.* It begins in the beginning and it stretches out over the years that follow. God commits to us. We commit to him and his leading. We trust him to select the very best parent for who our child will become. Over and over and over again.

I prayed for this child. *This* child. This *daughter.* This *Eva.* And I know that I know that I know that God heard my prayers. He gave my daughter the *best* mother for who she was, is, and will become. And he gave me the *best* daughter for who I was, am, and will become. I've committed to believe this. I've learned to trust it. I've worked to remember it. I've purposed to live it. All of it. For always.

....

My Lord God, I have no idea where I am going. I do not see the road ahead of me. I cannot know for certain where it will end. Nor do I really know myself, and the fact that I think I am following Your will does not mean that I am actually doing so. But I believe that the desire to please You does in fact please You. And I hope that I have that desire in all that I am doing. I hope that I will never do anything apart from that desire. And I know that if I do this You will lead me by the right road though I may know nothing about it. Therefore I will trust You always, though I may seem to be lost and in the shadow of death. I will not fear, for You are ever with me, and You will never leave me to face my perils alone.

—THOMAS MERTON[2]

Once

Once I had a girl—a daughter of my own. We were connected and yet apart.

Before setting eyes on her little baby being, I'd been cautioned that as much as I longed to give her all I'd never had, she would have already experienced the greatest wound of her life. I'd been warned that it would not be my soul but rather the soul of a stranger that would reflect back from her eyes.

Still, we bonded. I knew her heart, mind, and body. Until one day she turned away and left me with the stranger's silhouette. (Had she—the stranger—also experienced such a void?)

I realize now I may have loved her too much. Perhaps even made of her an idol. I meant no harm. I simply wanted to fill her emptiness to the rim. Or was it my own emptiness I sought to complete?

The punishment of her absence is painful. And then I realize you have missed her more than me. Before I dreamed dreams for her, you dreamed. Before I pictured her whole by my hand, you held her whole in yours. Before she turned from me, she had already turned from you. I didn't know. I had no inkling. You were already wounded, raw, rejected, grieving.

And still you hope. My wick smolders. My reediness bends to break. You stand and wait.

Help me, your daughter, to stand with you to wait for our daughter together.

5

Humility

It might seem that during the long season of my daughter's surprise pregnancy and her preterm birth to a baby needing extra care that I was magnanimously focused on *them*, free of concern for myself. Nope. Like most moms who think their kids would never go in such a direction, I flipped out. I didn't want my daughter to be pregnant. I didn't want to be a grandmother and Evan a grandfather. I didn't want my teenage son, a few years younger than my daughter, to suddenly become an uncle. No.

Even after Eva made her amazing decision to relinquish Thomas, even after God revealed his miraculously appointed adoptive parents, I didn't feel especially loved by God, nor did I want to live loved. I wanted to hide my daughter, my family, and myself. I didn't want to lead a mothering organization, involving myriad moms just setting out on the journey of motherhood, while making my way through what I defined as "ruin."

Underneath the surface of my coping, I wrestled with some all-about-me issues. I struggled with God—how could he let this happen? To *me*? I'd been such a good girl! My mother had been a mess. That was not my fault, I was beginning to understand through the layers and levels of counseling I received. But, still, she was a mess and her mess had affected me. I had determined I would mother better than she. And I had. I didn't get drunk. I kept a clean house. I was *there* with my kids: at their school conferences, at their swim meets, and for their everyday needs. The result? My daughter was now in a mess. What?

I need to say something that's hard for me to say. (Seriously— and this whole book hasn't been hard?) What I mean is, I need to talk about some stuff that I began to discover about myself near the beginning of our family's long ordeal but that I'm just now—years later—starting to understand. This "something" was more about who I am than what I did or didn't do.

I was beginning to discover I was proud.

Back in our ranch-style home in Houston, I had learned to survive my mother's instability by investing myself in managing my universe. Not only did I hammer away at trying to fix what was broken, I also put down stakes in new territories to make sure nothing else broke or even looked broken around me. Ever.

When my younger brother's friends came to play, I handled their parents, answering the front door and nudging my stumbling mother behind it while monitoring the pickup time. I weeded the front flower beds and painted the wrought-iron trim within reach. (The end result probably looked funny to anyone over five feet tall, but since I couldn't see any higher, I didn't notice.) I washed and ironed my clothes—in fact, most all of our clothes. I rearranged the furniture in our den and living room. I wiped the kitchen cabinets free of insect droppings and vacuumed our gold-hued carpet into neat rows of pile.

My mother's illness shaped my resilience. And much of my efforts were focused on doing life *better, right, obediently*. I had no idea that such a survival technique would rear its head as pride in my mothering of my own children—but oh mercy, it did. Big time.

When a friend revealed over coffee that her preteen son had punched a hole through the Sheetrock in their home, I rummaged through possible responses. On the surface I commiserated. He was a good kid—how could he be so *violent?* But beneath my sympathetic tone, I also determined that *no one* in our family would do such a thing. Underneath my care for her was a judgment: surely she and her husband were not parenting well.

A coworker's teen took their car without permission and brought it back dented. They didn't discover the bang-up—or the cause—for several weeks. I was incredulous. How could they not notice?

When a neighbor's daughter started acting out with boys five years older, I decided that those parents were just too permissive. The young girl would have been fine with stricter rules.

Elisa the Great Evaluator emerged. I hadn't realized I possessed this tendency to judge others. I'd thought of myself as vulnerable and compassionate and real. That was the persona I valued and the one I applied (I thought) each day. But mothering is a serious vocation demanding a deep investment that grows from a relentless conviction that we are *right*. It's tricky to be honest about ourselves—with ourselves—in the process.

Perhaps because my days were spent 24/7 in mothering matters—leading a mothering organization and then returning home to mother—I was extra-aware of the strong opinions that accompany mothering. Whether the issue is public, private, or homeschooling, working inside or outside the home, breastfeeding or bottle-feeding, styles of discipline, or the number of hours allotted for TV or computer—you name it—moms find themselves caught on the barbed wire of comparison with the choices of other moms. In my public platform, I had been extremely careful to steer wide of controversial topics that might leave some mom, any mom, feeling excluded from the arms of God and his people. MOPS International exists to reach *every* mother of preschoolers. In place of official statements on certain subjects, I offered what I thought was a vulnerable presentation of my own questionings, my own lacks, my own needs, and God's presence in them.

But within the walls of my own efforts, I actually thought I knew what I was doing.

To this day, I've never discovered any passion quite like the mothering passion. Mother-love is a love of an intensity that has surprised me. For sure, there is the fact that mother-love is tied to a child that is under our care for its very survival. Yikes! But I've also discovered that mother-love is intrinsically about *me* as the mother, because fundamentally, it's not just what I *do* that matters—the results of what I do become who I *am*. And *I* was determined to do motherhood *right*.

In the days of Eva's pregnancy with Thomas, God took me deep—and then deeper—into these previously untapped assumptions. He used friends and Scripture and books, like Brennan Manning's *The Ragamuffin Gospel*, and therapy—*lots* of therapy—until I began to face a truth I'd never seen as something negative: most of my life I'd been working at being *special—better—above the mess.*

In my childhood I tried to fix my first family with my scrubbing and painting and managing and *adulting* the lives around me. While my efforts surely helped us all survive, in the end they didn't and couldn't work because I wasn't an adult and it wasn't my mess to fix.

But in the process of trying, I mistakenly concluded that I, myself, wasn't broken. I couldn't be. Further, I believed I could gain love by being special, better, above the mess. Tenacious Elisa. Survivor Elisa. Mature Elisa. Special Elisa. I liked this

identity and wrapped it around me like a superhero cape, swirling it through my teen, then young adult, then professional, then
mothering days. In many ways it (again) worked. After all, there is
so much special in each of us. God's unique DNA, invested in our
very creation, results in one-of-a-kind offerings each of us grows
to give. And my particular gifts were culturally approved, socially
charming, and platform worthy. God made me good at lots of
things, especially the kind of leadership that others like to follow.

With Eva's foray into choices that led to pregnancy, now I
felt *human* like everyone else, at least as a mother. Small fragments of my carefully crafted Special Elisa began to fracture.

I track my processing from my journal entries that year:

January 11: I told my stepmother about Eva. She said, "I always
knew you were too good and that something awful would
happen to you." *(See—Special Elisa!)*

January 15: I told my sister. She cried. *(See—Special again!)*

Then I begin to crack . . .

February 1: People carry around so much pain! There are
people in pain all around us all the time.

February 5: We go to family counseling. The counselor has us
stand in a circle and tell each other what we believe we need
to hear. We tell Eva, "Don't be afraid." We tell Ethan, "Don't
bottle it up." We tell Evan, "It's not your fault." They tell me,
"I love you."

Did I believe that? That I was loved? Special Elisa might be
loved. But . . . the rest of me? The part I had pushed down and
hidden—denied. The broken, imperfect me?

I start to own my own mess. My sin is no better than anyone else's. Maybe I'm successful in ministry and doing a good job in the role to which God has called me. Maybe I'm not a drunk like my mother was. Maybe I haven't abandoned my family as my father did. Maybe I only leaned into the "special" category as a means of coping with childhood pain. But my sin is still sin: my sin is that I think I can be above sin.

My sin is pride.

One afternoon I returned from a counseling appointment to my bedroom and closed the door. I teetered on the edge of some raw crevice in my being. I didn't really want to go there: down. But the effort of clinging to the side of the cliff was becoming too difficult.

I grabbed my Bible and journal. I'd been reading in Luke and opened up to chapter 7—the story of the "sinful" woman. At first I didn't relate. I didn't see myself as sinful. It was everyone else who was sinful—*they* were the problem.

I read and then reread Jesus' words to the woman in verse 47: "I tell you that her many sins are forgiven, so she showed great love. But the person who is forgiven only a little will love only a little."

Something shifted in me. We love little when we've been forgiven little. And then: the more we're forgiven, the more we're able to love.

I flipped to underlined sentences in *The Ragamuffin Gospel*— "Repentance is not what we do in order to earn forgiveness; it is what we do because we have been forgiven."[1] "Forgiveness precedes repentance."[2]—and I slowly understood that until we are forgiven, we don't really understand what it is we have to be repentant of.

One more zinger: "Many of us *pretend to believe* we are sinners. Consequently, all we can do is pretend to believe we have been forgiven."[3] Ugh.

I began to see that God had allowed just the right chink in my armor of specialness: mother shame. I wasn't "enough" after all. I was never intended to be enough: good enough, all-powerful enough, special enough. "Enoughness" wasn't within my grasp, nor was it God's goal for my life. God so desires that we embrace and accept our not-enoughness—because then we see our need for him. Going further, I surely wasn't better-than. All around me were moms and dads doing a hugely better job than me. At least their kids seemed to look better.

I'd soldiered through this and that and the other to make it this far in my maze of survival. It was time to surrender to my own need. I could follow the logic now. If I surrendered, I would discover God's provision of love for me. If I saw my need to be forgiven, I would see my need for his love. If I saw my need for his love, I would let him love me. And then I would know that I am, indeed, loved.

Right?

I was still stuck. It's so hard to give way when our heels have been dug in deep in resistance. Just to survive. Honestly the only way I gave in was bit by bit, through one conscious choice after another. One inch at a time, I looked and saw my need. One step at a time, I admitted who I wasn't. One day at a time, I allowed God into places I never knew existed in me, and spots I never imagined he wanted to enter with me.

Gradually, God grew in me a new acceptance of my true need for him. I began to understand that when I embrace forgiveness—and therefore enable myself to receive God's love for me—then I'm actually *more* useful for God's kingdom purposes. How many of us judge ourselves as disqualified for ministry due to what we have endured! When really, our messiness, handed to God for redemption, actually qualifies us for further use.

In those redefining days, I met with my board chair at MOPS, mortified at my newly owned brokenness. His response?

"What would we rather have: a president who's 'doing fine,' or one who's even more equipped to address our target audience?" And not long after, a MOPS leader told me, "If you resign, you tell the world that your children's choices are your fault. How does that empower moms?"

I'm not done yet—even today. The yielding has continued long and hard over the years. It's not easy to relinquish a survival technique so long employed and so successfully engaged.

In Richard Rohr's *Falling Upward*, I discovered an analogy that loosened yet a few more strongholds of my proud defense. In post–World War II Japan, elder soldiers struggled to reenter civilian life. The only identity they knew was that of being a loyal soldier to their country. To relieve these souls, Japanese communities created a ritual where a soldier was publicly thanked and praised for his service to the people. Then they were formally released from duty and charged to return to their role as citizen, as normal human being.[4]

Alice Miller calls this over-functioning role "the gifted child" in her insightful book *The Drama of the Gifted Child*. Her point is that intuitive, survivor children employ a gifting to protect themselves from further wounding through their resilient emotional capacity.[5] (I'd read this book back in the earliest days of my journey but couldn't get past her description of the "gifted child." Not me! I'm not "gifted!" And so I couldn't access her wisdom.)

It's taken a lifetime for me to understand—and gradually own—my neediness. And over a decade to embrace my need for humility in parenting. First I swallowed the tonic that formulaic parenting would achieve success for me as a mother. Next I gulped down the false teaching that my efforts could make up for the sins—and brokenness—of others around me. And then I drank deeply from the lie that the "specialness" that helped me survive would eventually save me from my own sins.

Instead I lift another cup to my lips and sip from Anne

Lamott's observation: "Our bottled charm is the main roadblock to drinking that clear cool glass of love."[6]

I stumbled upon a book that offered its own kind of "love dare": spend ten minutes each day thinking about the fact that God loves you.[7] I thought I'd give it a try. The first few days I barely made it thirty seconds before the day's tasks distracted me. By the third day, I'd forced myself to five minutes. Nothing happened, likely because all I was focused on was if I was doing the exercise "right."

Trying again, I sat and thought—and *boing!*—into my mind came a sentence, first person, God to me.

I love you, Elisa.

I'd never heard that before. I'd heard, "Jesus loves you." "God loves you." "You are loved." But I'd never heard this: *I love you, Elisa.* The words seeped into me where I sat in my chair, tethering me in place in a security I'd never before considered possible.

I love you, Elisa.

Wow!

Today I tattoo on my heart the truth, *I love you, Elisa.* God's love makes me special. Unique. Fearfully and wonderfully made. That specialness does not exempt me from being human—and (say it) broken. But it does ensure that I am loved *just the way I am.* When I cling to my perceived righteousness, I miss the adoration of the One who made me in his image but still loves me when I'm way less than he imagined. So, I—Elisa Made Special by God's Love—embrace my fallenness, understanding that by doing so, I am free to receive God's love.

I release my loyal Soldier Elisa from duty. She bravely offered herself on the childhood altar of survival that I might live. I acknowledge the "gifted child" who rose up and beyond and took me above with her, out of the tumult of my original family. And . . . bless her heart . . . I thank Special Elisa. She gave me life when no other person could do so. Their time is past.

They couldn't—and can't—give me what I need as an adult, as a human in need of help from God.

None of us is exempt from the startling reality of suffering in and around us because we have lived our lives "right." In fact, doing life "right" can miss the mark as much as failure when we pride ourselves on our right living.

Judge not. Good words for Elisa the Great Evaluator twenty years ago and today. Good words for all of us. Because in judging others, we leave ourselves open to the ruin we cannot avoid—with no hope of rescue. As my pastor preached, "Oh, how careful we have to be when we begin to exclude people from the presence of God because we end up disqualifying ourselves."[8]

I embrace the broken family value of humility. Yes, "it" (whatever "it" is!) can and may happen to me. I am deeply loved by God, *yet* I am not exempt from pain, tragedy, hardship, or error just because I'm trying to obey God. And I'm not better than anyone else by my attempts to do so.

There are a few now-repaired holes in our Sheetrock and dents in my car that remind me—just in case I forget.

....

Salvation is not sin perfectly avoided, as the ego would prefer; but in fact, salvation is sin turned on its head and used in our favor.

—RICHARD ROHR[9]

Space

There's too much of it all of a sudden: space. Its creation has been painful, the fullness tearing out from my clutching fingers, splaying the contents I'd held so tightly. Now my hands are empty.

Two upstairs bedrooms yawn empty, stripped of their occupants and their belongings. I close the doors.

Downstairs, a newly finished basement spreads itself from wall to wall. I place a few glasses on the shelves above the new sink. A coffeemaker on the counter even though I don't plan to brew any. An item goes in the art niche: some horse weather vane thing I found years ago. It'll do. The leftover summer geraniums I pull in from the walk-out patio.

Blank boxes gape on my calendar. A vacant passenger seat in my car. Sparse offerings in my refrigerator and pantry.

While desperately uncomfortable with the new emptiness in my days, I can't bring myself to fill up the space. It's too soon. Too new. I don't know it well enough.

This isn't normal for me. Normal for me is to fill space the second it appears. Garages. Basements. Spare rooms. Attics. Bookshelves. Chairs around my table. Until clutter overtakes even the corners and there is no more. Space. I spend my space on me and mine before even thinking of you, God.

But I can't fill this space. This has been a season of emptying. Of moving out what used to be within my walls. And I'm not sure what is to go there next.

Christmas approaches. You whisper to me to leave the space as it is. To let you make even more of it. That you are to be the occupant. That you have made—and will make—more space in my home, in my work, in my marriage, and in my mothering because you know that I will need places for more of you in these days.

"People never pour new wine into old leather bags. Otherwise, the bags will break, the wine will spill, and the wine bags will be ruined. But people always pour new wine into new wine bags. Then both will continue to be good" (Matthew 9:17).

And then:

"Because there were no rooms left in the inn, she wrapped the baby with pieces of cloth and laid him in a feeding trough" (Luke 2:7).

It's been about space since the beginning, hasn't it? How did *you* fit into a womb? A baby? A carpenter's body? A tomb? You did so that you might communicate more clearly, be more tangibly one of us. And we couldn't even make room for you then.

6

Courage

My daughter was courageous and committed to choose the *best* for her son. After the momentous, life-altering advent and release of Thomas, I expected life to return to normal. I looked ahead and imagined the cracks in our days healed and whole. I projected myself telling the story of such goodness, with no more missteps and woundings.

I was wrong.

After Thomas was safely situated in his new home, we all wondered about our next step. Evan focused on work, me on MOPS, both of us on Ethan, and Eva pointed herself toward school.

Eva wasn't ready, though. Her very being was fragmented and she struggled to put the pieces back together. Instead of school, she ended up in a relationship with a man seven years older, allowing him first to control and then . . . to abuse her. In a counseling session where Evan and I had determined to "tough love" her away from him, we sat stunned as she told us that she preferred him to us and would be leaving our home for his.

After all I've done for you? Are you crazy? If I could have *willed* her home, I would have. We'd been through Thomas together! How could she choose to leave us—the loving parents who had stood by her no matter what?

But out the door she went. To him. Away from us.

The tug-of-war for her life began. Friends prayed earnestly: against Satan, for God, against lies and deceit, for truth. One night she relented and Evan went and got her. The next day she returned. It went on for months. I remember one night after a short visit I dropped her off at the hovel where she lived, and my heart screamed for her to stay with me, not to get out of the car. She stared into my eyes, *home* reflected there. I fought to remain neutral: no pressure, no strings, only hope. She wavered. She said she wanted to leave where she was, but she didn't know where she would go.

Stay quiet. I worked to be still. I knew the choice had to be *hers.* She cried at her own lostness, torn between the all-too-familiar hell and the now-unfamiliar home. And then she pulled away. While I sat helplessly, she gathered her things, retraced her steps up the path to the porch, unlocked the front door, and returned.

Thanksgiving went by. She called to ask how to mash potatoes. We met for a Christmas dinner in a restaurant and gave her the present of a warm coat. Finally Evan and I knew that unless we stopped communicating with Eva, she'd never feel the consequences of her choices and would never have the clarity she needed to choose what she really wanted. We met Eva at a restaurant. I think I ordered a Diet Coke. She looked at us with her gorgeous, wide eyes—her body unnaturally thin. We didn't know it then but thyroid disease was having its way in her. Using word pictures that had been suggested by the counselor, we told her that we'd done all we could do for her.

Evan described her choices feeling to him like a Grand

Canyon that he couldn't scale. He needed to push his chair just a bit back from the edge. It was too hard to watch her "fall."

I told her I felt like a trapeze artist. We had swung out with her, preparing her for her future, holding her until the appropriate transition "bar" was within her reach. But she let go of us before the next healthy handhold appeared, and I couldn't reach far enough to go with her.

Evan asked her to call him once a week to let him know she was okay and instructed her not to call me at all, that it was too hard for us to watch her do this to her life. Evan told her that when she was ready to leave the man, she could call and he would come get her whenever and wherever and get her to some help. Out of state. Away from danger.

She blinked in surprise, expecting us to take back our words. When we didn't, she swallowed, said she understood, and left. Her eighteenth birthday passed and we held our breath, fearing that the day would end with her married to this man.

Late one afternoon as I left the MOPS office I saw her walking from the bus stop. (Stunningly, the run-down house where they lived was just blocks from where I worked.) She saw me and ran to my car. I unrolled the window and held my hand on the key, ready to start the ignition. She put her hand on the windowsill and I saw one nail left on her always-manicured hands. God heart-whispered, *When all the nails are gone . . . she'll be back.*

We chatted. *How's it going? You look okay. Take care.* And I drove away, watching her walk off in my rearview mirror.

A few days later, she stood at the doorway of my office and said, "I'm ready, Mom." As I drew in a breath and prayed for wisdom, she sat down across from me and revealed that her boyfriend made her leave the house every morning at six, and then she had to walk until her job started at ten and couldn't go back home until evening. And that he beat her.

I looked at her hands. There were no nails left.

Eva got help. Evan flew her to a special center where we all learned how traumatic it can be for some adopted children to absorb their own identity. Our family joined in her treatment—now *our* treatment. We learned that adoptees face different identity issues than biological children and that it is not uncommon for adopted teens to become pregnant.

We certainly weren't the only parents in pain in our less-than-tidy world. My dearest friend and coauthor discovered her daughter had alopecia as a senior in high school. Long locks of beautiful blonde hair clumped on her pillow when it should have graced her gorgeous head. She wore a wig through athletic events, through choir concerts, and to her senior prom. Her self-image was shattered and her mom hovered to catch the pieces.

The marriage of dear friends in our small group crumbled. Another friend was diagnosed with stomach cancer. Colorado endured the Columbine massacre. How do any of us find the courage to lift our heads?

I read in the paper of a man caring 24/7 for his thirty-five-year-old, brain-damaged son. Oh, the pain! Yet his take on his adult child's life seared me: "He's injured. He's wounded, but there is something we can share that's beautiful and learning to recognize that beauty, well it's something you have to experience. Once you see it, you see the world differently."[1]

I remember one night praying in thankfulness and tears, relieved that the ordeal had passed. My heart reached up toward hope, yet not free of fear. I prayed, tongue in cheek, "You're not going to get me now, God, are you? Now that I think the bad has passed, you're not going to allow *more*, are you?"

....

Eva began to recover from the trauma of Thomas's birth and the aftermath as well as from the choices she'd made as her way of coping. She moved back home, went to school to get her hairstyling license, continued in counseling, and began to make her way.

Until one November night, when driving in the early hours with a friend, her life changed yet again.

I awoke on the West Coast. With my coworker in another bedroom, I was staying in the guest home of a MOPS board member. We'd flown out for a MOPS event to take place that evening. I looked at the clock: 6:02 a.m. Then I reached for my phone. In those days I turned it off each night, not wanting to be disturbed by a late-night call. Never again.

There were six missed calls—all from Evan. The message light blinked. I punched the button and listened while pulling back the covers and opening the door from the bedroom to the hall to see if Janis was up yet. She was—making coffee in the townhome's kitchen.

As she looked up to offer a morning greeting, I collapsed on the floor, howling. Evan's recorded words rattled through me, and I tried to get them out as Janis rushed over.

There had been an accident. Eva had been behind the wheel. She was in the hospital. Someone else was severely hurt—maybe dead. The second message: he died. A friend of Eva's we didn't know. Call. Come home.

Tears of sympathy appeared in Janis' eyes. We'd known each other for years by now, and she'd seen much of me and my family. In my gut I *knew* the worst: there had been an accident. Someone was dead. Somewhere parents were keening in grief. My daughter's life would once again be changed forever.

On the plane home—just hours after all the missed calls and messages, I picked up a book I'd been reading. I'm sure that in my own way, I was in some kind of shock. The writer talked about how women can grow anesthetized to their feelings and their lives. And then she shared some words from a short story she had penned. They jarred me . . . *Really, God?*

I was reading the book *The Dance of the Dissident Daughter*, specifically a section where the author, Sue Monk Kidd, describes the first fictional story she ever wrote:

"People deposit their misery somewhere in their body," the character Hallie says. "Mine apparently is in the sleep center of my brain." But despite her awareness that her sleepwalking signals something wrong in her life, she refuses to face her life or her problems.

Then one night she sleepwalks outside and climbs a ladder that has been left leaning against the house. She wakes three rungs from the top, everything around her darkness and air. Frightened, she backs down and returns to her room, where she ties her arm to the bedpost, afraid she'll sleepwalk again and wake on the roof, this time stepping off into thin air.

But even then she doesn't confront the changes she needs to make. So she walks in her sleep again, this time backing the car down the driveway and crashing into a Japanese elm. It takes the crash to wake her. She sits at the wheel, stunned, a trickle of blood on her forehead, knowing finally that she must alter the direction of her life.

Here is one of the principles of women waking: If you don't respond to the first gentle nudges, they will increase in intensity. Next you will wake up on the roof. And if you do not respond to that, there will likely be a crash. There are women who sleep through the crashes, too. I imagine by then the impulse to wake gives up and they drift into permanent hibernation.[2]

By the time I landed, Evan had brought Eva home from the hospital. Her injuries were a broken clavicle and a concussion. But her friend had not survived. They were the only two in the car, in the accident.

I feared for Eva's future as never before. My daughter. My beautiful, courageous, wonderful daughter. What in the world lay ahead for her? And how would God work in even this for her good?

In our family room, Evan and I challenged Eva to reevaluate her life—who was guiding her, to what was she yielding? Gently, but firmly, we begged her to realign with God. If the days ahead were to reveal the course for her life ahead—legally and practically—didn't she want to make sure she was yielding to God's power in and through it?

Evan and I moved to the adjoining kitchen to prepare a meal and to leave her alone with her thoughts. "I did it," she softly said from her chair.

"What?" I asked.

"Prayed," she answered. "God's in charge, not me."

And so Eva's life went on. So did ours. Together.

....

An answer to prayer. I reflected, *Why do we try to cocoon our children from the lives they live—from the very things that led us to Christ ourselves—from sin? Eventually, isn't it sin—their sin, all of our sin— that makes us want Jesus?*

Yet, I was so weary. My journal shows the fray within me:

July 7: I sit here. Paralyzed. Frozen. Wincing at the sky as I await the next and the next and the next blow to my world. The deconstruction of Elisa. Could it become the reconstruction?

I have no words.

All I can do is describe the weariness. The tired arms and legs and heart. My lungs won't even fill anymore. Too much effort. Not enough space. I'm filled with tears, down to my torso. Drowning in them. But they don't emerge.

A friend sent a note: "As I read John Eldredge on our relationship to God, I kept thinking of yours with Eva. Such pain, such love, such longing. And, of course, God feels as you do, with the power of infinity."

He enclosed the quote:

God's relationship with us and our world is just that: a *relationship*. As with every relationship, there's a certain amount of unpredictability and the ever-present likelihood that you'll get hurt. The ultimate risk anyone ever takes is to love, for as C. S. Lewis says, "Love anything and your heart will be wrung and possibly broken. If you want to make sure of keeping it intact, you must give it to no one, not even an animal." But God does give it, again and again and again, until he is literally bleeding from it all.[3]

There were legal matters to settle—that took months. Was it years? In the middle of them Eva asked me to go to the doctor with her. She felt weird. We met there. On the way I'd felt a tug . . . of what, I'm not sure. God? I pushed it away.

In the examination room, we waited for the doctor. Eva had completed the normal prep, blood pressure, urine test, temperature, pulse, etc. The doctor knocked and opened the door. We'd known her for years, as she'd been our doctor since Eva was an infant. I felt her nervousness—not normal for her.

She looked at Eva and then at me and plunged ahead, "Well, the news is in. You're pregnant!" Then, "Is that a good thing?"

Eva offered a quick smile, clearly delighted. I tasted something sour in my mouth, and the doctor's voice went mute to me. In its place came questions that I kept to myself: *Huh? Again? What will she do this time?*

Walking to the car, I asked some of these unuttered queries. Eva was thrilled. She'd always wanted a baby. Nineteen and nearly twenty now, she would work this out. She wanted me to be happy. Honestly? I wasn't. I think I probably lectured her as she headed to her own car and back to work and I went home.

In my bedroom—actually, I think I collapsed in my bathroom by the bathtub—I was alone with the news. The cold tile under my knees beckoned me. I lay down with my face on it. Evan was out of cell range at the time. Of course she was pregnant. I remembered the words of the counselor from months prior: "Adoptees often rework their pain by giving birth . . ." While I could wrap my head around such a rational explanation, *still* I struggled with what her pregnancy would mean for our family. For me. I turned my face toward heaven and was very clear with God about the *not-nowness* of this moment. *Really, God?*

In a heart-whisper, he responded, *It's a life, Elisa. This is not about loss. This is about life.*

I gathered courage from the air around my feet. I prayed that Eva would somehow be redeemed by this birth. After all, aren't we all redeemed by a birth? One spectacular display of God coming forth?

Slowly, the numbness wore off and feeling returned. A tinge of happiness bubbled in my soul and spread. I *would* be a grandmother. Evan *would* be a grandfather. Ethan *would* be an uncle. It was growing to be good. Soon it would be *very* good.

Eva joined a MOPS group. We celebrated the upcoming life with a baby shower, with nursery decor, with doctor's visits and an on-time, safe arrival.

Eva gave birth to an amazing baby boy. We joyed over his arrival in a hospital room filled with balloons and flowers and friends and family. The adventure home started bumpily when just minutes after Eva was situated in her nursery upstairs—the same, dreamed-about room for Eva with a room next door for the baby—Marcus suddenly stopped breathing and we had to call 911. After a few days in the hospital and tests that a newborn, and a mother recovering from a C-section, should never have to endure, Marcus came home with a prescription for reflux and oxygen for a condition called periodic breathing.

In the novel *Cutting for Stone*, the main character, Hema, is a woman, doctor, and adoptive mother. When she meets the biological father of her twin boys and is challenged on her need to be by the bedside of her dying son, she pushes back, "These are my sons. They are a gift given to me. The pain, the heartbreak, if there is to be heartbreak, are all mine—that comes with the gift. I am their mother."[4] Yes. I was learning to love my daughter in the pain and the heartbreak as well as in the joy.

Eva and Marcus lived upstairs in our house for nearly three years before they met and married faithful, loving Jason and became a new family unit. Marcus is my grand*one*. He calls me Yia Yia and Evan is BeePeez. (It would take another few pages to explain this!) He is the most perfect gift God could have ever created for me. God has used Marcus to grow me into more of me, more than I ever thought possible.

I so admire Eva's mothering instincts. Her keen understanding of what her son needs guides her decisions with him. Her fierce advocacy of his world protects him from the unwanted in life. I love her strong selfhood, how clear she is with her opinions, the passion she holds for what she holds dear.

Courage, parent. God knows what your children are about. He knit your children together in their mother's womb—perhaps yours, perhaps the womb of another—but nevertheless, he knit them. Before a word is on their tongues, he knows it. He has numbered their days. He knows their comings and goings.

And God knows you. He will not try you beyond what you are able to bear. There is no "off" ramp in parenting. Instead of looking for it, take courage and parent with an attitude that yields to the seemingly impossible. You may be shocked by the realities you face, but parenting calls you to continue. And in the continuing, you will likely discover, as I did, that God will grow more of you, more for you, more in you.

....

And now, GOD, do it again—
  bring rains to our drought-stricken lives
So those who planted their crops in despair
  will shout hurrahs at the harvest,
So those who went off with heavy hearts
  will come home laughing, with armloads of blessing.

—PSALM 126:4–6 MSG

Door

There is such emptiness.

An empty house.

An empty room.

An empty bed.

A car that should have been filled with her laughter, her music, her perfume, her errands, her life.

A bathroom that should overflow with steam from her showers. Wastebaskets empty of her discard. Closets and drawers yawning bare.

And my heart, which has given her up. She didn't move out from there. No, I simply shut the door when she left, looking for another life. When she was gone, I closed the once-always-open door.

Now I look at its backside, an unfamiliar, hopeless face that allows no view past its barricade. I stretch my sight down the road to what might one day still be.

I hope she knows, when she glances back at it—if she happens to—that it is not locked.

7

Reality

My first garden was in a Dixie cup. My kindergarten teacher passed out Dixie cups, marigold seeds, and then troweled mounds of dark soil out into each of our "flower pots." Tiny servings of water were added to our dirt to create what looked like mud to me. Finally she instructed us to gently punch the marigold seed down into the dirt.

I took it home, carefully cupping the tiny garden in my chubby fingers until I safely arrived and lodged it on the windowsill where it would have a good view of the sun.

Each morning I sprang from my bed to check its progress. It always looked the same to me: brown, muddy dirt in a cup. Faithfully, I watered it. Loyally, I turned it so that all sides would have equal exposure to the sun and the view from the window.

But each day, my inspection of its progress revealed nothing. Zip. My garden was just brown dirt in a cup.

One morning, I ran to the cup, just as I had so many other mornings, and found nothing but brown dirt in a cup. I'd grabbed my mother's hand, tugged her over to the cup, and with a pout begged, "Can I dig up my seed to see what it's doing down there in the dirt?"

My mother wisely responded, "Elisa, you can dig it up, but if you do, it'll stop growing and you'll ruin it. You have to give seeds time to grow, and you can't get in their way."

There have been moments—make that whole seasons— when the Dixie cup garden of my son looked to me like so much dirt in a cup.

Ethan's name means "steadfast heart." And from early on, it fit. Ethan was the type to grab hold of something and then take it apart in order to understand it better. An old toaster. A telephone we'd unplugged and were no longer using. When handed a flashlight, he didn't just turn it on and off; he unscrewed it, removed the batteries, and then started after the little metal spring doohickey that conducted the charge.

His steadfastness reached out relationally as well. With his dad. With his sister. And with me, his mom. I remember one night when he was about six, he called me into his bedroom just before lights-out. In those days he slept on the top bunk of his bunk set. As I entered his room, I took in his boney bare shoulders (he slept in boxers only), his towheaded gleam, and the extremely sincere expression on his face.

"Mom, I want to tell you something, but I'm a little afraid," he began.

"Why, Boodle?"

"Well, it's kinda hard."

"Okay, wanna give it a try?"

"Okay—but it's a lot."

"Take a deep breath," I offered, wondering just what he'd been up to.

He leaned a bit over the bed rail, grabbed my hands in his, took a deep breath, and then, looking straight into my eyes, sang what I recognized as "You Are So Beautiful to Me." All the words. All the stanzas. He ran the last words together in an effort to be done with getting it out: "You aresobeautifulto me."

Tears sprang in my eyes. I squeezed his hands and told him, "That's beautiful, Ethan. *You* are beautiful! I love you so." He smiled and scooted under his covers but not before I made out that one adorable dimple in his right cheek. My boy.

I have loved this child, now man, with an everlasting love since the second he was mine, which was at about thirteen days of age. We got the call from the agency that our baby boy was ready the day before a Morgan family reunion. Ethan came right along with us, the newest Morgan, celebrated and folded into our family. When all the families packed and left, Eva, now nearly three and clearly confused, asked, "When does *he* leave?" and pointed to her new brother.

Ethan was an easy child. He rode on my hip and enjoyed whatever I enjoyed wherever I enjoyed it.

When his older sister went off to kindergarten, Ethan and I created our own adventures. He'd hide in the clothing racks while I shopped until I looked up to find him missing. Moments later I'd hear over the loudspeaker, "Mrs. Morgan, please come to the guest desk to retrieve your son. He's lost you." How could he *always* find the guest counter and he could *never* find me?

We lunched at a neighborhood Chinese restaurant where he ordered egg rolls and fried rice and we giggled while wrestling rice between our chopsticks and held contests over who could endure the most hot mustard before our brains crawled out of our skulls.

In the summer, he spent hours in the backyard, clad in shorts, T-shirt, and snow boots with his blankie tied about his shoulders Superman-style and a winter cap—with ear warmers— on his head. Playground gravel was his currency. He carried it about in his pockets. He brought it indoors in his foamy boots. He stuck it in his cheeks and wobbled from slide to swing and then—*oops!*—plopped down in between, unintentionally swallowing his treasure. I once found the entire sprinkler turn-on pipe filled with gravel from one of his excursions.

Early in his life, Ethan knew about Jesus with a heart-knowing. He accompanied me to see my nail tech friend and played under the table while she polished my nails. Back home after one such visit, we couldn't find his toy binoculars. We searched all over our house until he grabbed my hand, spun me around, and reminded me, "Mommy, Jesus knows where my b'noculars are. Let's ask him to show us!" He bowed his head expecting me to pray—so I did, following his lead. Just hours later my friend called and asked if Ethan might have left a pair of red binoculars at her shop when we were there.

Once, he exited the shower, threw his chest out with bravado, and for no specific reason pronounced, "Jesus Christ is the Son of God who died on the cross for our sins!" In first grade when a classmate was over playing and asked Ethan about the cross he wore about his neck (a souvenir from the summer camp he attended), Ethan told him all about Jesus and how his friend ought to invite him into his heart.

....

Than: pronounced "Ton," which rhymes with *son*. That's what I called Ethan. Still do. My Than.

Beneath the sunny surface of my son, little worries niggled. Before the bathroom mirror each morning, he'd splash water over his hair, wetting it down and combing it into a neat, dark cap. Dark. His hair was blond as could be but when it was wet, it shone with a brown gloss. "Why do you wet down your hair, Than?" I asked one morning. "Because I like to look like you and Eva and Dad. And you all have dark hair."

Okay.

When Ethan discovered swimming, it was the breaststroke that he owned. After experiencing a few disqualifications because he'd lost focus and hadn't made it to the starting block on time, he pushed himself to master the stroke and became a Junior Olympian.

Bottom line? Ethan was a normal kid. Really. There was hardly anything that would cause concern to a parent. He moved through life with quiet ease.

Perhaps the first crack appeared, running nearly head to toe down the world of my son, when Evan and I held a family meeting to let Ethan know Eva was pregnant. He sat on the fireplace hearth in our family room in a very cool outfit of black jeans, a black shirt, and black shoes. Quite elegant for a thirteen-year-old. And then, as the news sunk in, so did his disposition. He was angry. He ran out the back door, letting it slam behind him. He was gone for hours. We searched and hollered and prayed. At last Eva said she'd go to find him and did, bringing him home.

We all sat back down again, promising each other that we'd make it through this time as a family, but we could all see the shift in Ethan's being. A darkness that would remain for a long time.

As Eva's stomach grew, Ethan's anger built. Looking back, he had a right to be angry. His sister had interrupted his world—his every day and, seemingly, his future. More painful, she had traipsed before him the very reality of his own beginning: he was the child of a teen mom Eva's current age. A mother who had decided that mothering him was not the best option for either of them. He didn't want to go there.

In my routine cleanings of his room, I discovered some unfamiliar items. A pipe? A lighter? The evidence revealed Ethan was smoking pot. Evan and I engaged a counselor for him. More layers laid out. Ethan was having trouble in school. Ethan was drinking. Ethan was skipping school. Ethan went to church and had a decent set of friends and sat at the dinner table and watched *Survivor* with the family. But Ethan was leaving Ethan and the rest of us, a little more all the time.

When I looked over the edge of the Dixie cup garden of his life, I saw a weed growing where I was sure I had planted a healthy seed promising a sturdy plant.

The day I numbingly accompanied Eva through Thomas's arrival, Evan drove to pick Ethan up from school. The three of us were certainly not prepared for all we were facing, and neither was Ethan. That night at the hospital, while Evan had gone to check on Thomas at the other hospital and I vigiled with Eva in her room, Ethan sat on a couch in the waiting room alone. When Evan returned, he sat down next to Ethan, taking in his deep sadness and the pool of tears on the tile floor around his feet.

Looking back, I'm not sure that Evan and I really grasped our son's torment. While we surely knew he was hurting and we stretched in every way we knew to meet his needs, I look back now and see our naïveté. I also see in his pain his deep-rooted efforts to grow, though frustrated by the environment about him.

What do I wish I'd done differently? It's so hard to know what to do when we are in the middle of the mist. Later we may have the clarity of its clearing. In the haze, we do well to survive.

Life hammered down on us. All of us. The months of grandparenting Thomas. Eva's spiraling down from herself in the abusive relationship. Then our family's loss of her from our lives. Ethan's world teetered. More trouble at school. A blip with road rage. More evidence of substance abuse in his room. We took away his driver's license. We held back his cell phone. He was grounded and fined and sequestered and you name it. Finally, we made him an offer: Would he agree to participate in a time of extended help, to remove him from the life he had been creating? In tears, he agreed. He, too, wanted to change.

As I drove my son to the airport to put him on a plane to a

safe place, my heart broke. Weren't we just deepening any issues
of abandonment for him? What were we thinking? We would
have only letters now for the next several weeks. How would I
know how my son was doing? If this last effort was working? If
he would be "fixed"? Would our family ever be *whole*?

To make matters even more emotional for me, I was headed
out that very day for a speaking engagement. I felt like a giant
fake—and yet God kept directing me along the way.

I wrote in my journal:

August 5: I had an image of birth last night—of a baby within
a womb struggling, pushing, clawing, poking to get out. He
even pushed against his mother's pelvis (mine?), reshaping,
breaking bone and tearing skin. All to get out.

Our kids are "reborn" from us with such violence! Is it
because their first birth was from the womb of another? Is it
because they must push through the adoption identity to find
their own?

October 21: I confess I am so cynical. I hear my words and
cringe. I'm angry. Why on earth would you ask me to minister from such depletion? What cues am I missing? Should I
stop speaking altogether? Or is this doubt from Satan? What
needs to change in me to cope with this?

I know you have been amazingly faithful. Ethan is in a
good place where he can get the help he needs. As a dear family friend and spiritual leader prays, I also pray, May he cry
from his heart and not just weep from his bed (Hosea 7:14).

But my day-to-day missing Ethan whispered to my heart,
He's not just out of my reach; he's lost! At church one Sunday I bowed
my head over my Bible. My pastor was preaching from John 1—
how Jesus knew where Nathanael was before Philip even talked

with him about following Jesus. I tried to read the text. My vision blurred. Tears? Maybe. More like the blur of disbelief. I was just plain spent. No hope happening here.

I focused my eyes again and read, "Nathanael asked, 'How do you know me?' Jesus answered, 'I saw you when you were under the fig tree, before Philip told you about me'" (John 1:48). I lifted my head and in my heart knew that just as Jesus *knew* where Nathanael was, he *knew* where Ethan was. I might not be able to see my son, but he was in plain sight to God.

I looked down at my feet. Then at the feet of a toddler sitting next to me. I realized I kept trying to put my feet into Ethan's shoes. Eva's. I wanted to walk for them. God gently said, *Elisa, you can't walk in their shoes. Only they can. Keep your feet in your own shoes.*

I tried.

I wrote a letter to Ethan upon his graduation from the out-of-state program:

> As I look back over your life, I have seen you discover *you* again and again, only to decide that you don't want *you* for some reason. I watch your potential sprout and then you drown it out.
>
> As you prepare to come home, it is clear that we still have much to work out together. You are different. I am different. Your dad and your sister are different. Our family is different. Each of us has changed. It will take commitment and communication to fully enjoy what we can together. And patience. And humor. And finding the middle ground together.
>
> Ethan, bring home who you've become and what you've learned. All of you and all of it.

Ethan returned. Bit by bit our family faced the reality that we were *all* different by what we had experienced individually and together.

I remember a season when MOPS was facing a brutal financial turn. Bills were large. Income was scarce. One coworker mouthed a mantra that I didn't like at first but grew to appreciate: "Reality is our friend. It bites, but it's our friend." Embracing reality with its ugly facts and figures brought our organization out of the slide and back to fruitfulness. The truth may be ugly, but in the end, it is a good thing.

In his book *Reaching for the Invisible God*, Philip Yancey writes of our nonnegotiable need to embrace reality. "God can forgive any sin, and can deal with any spiritual condition. We fall down, we get up. Fall down, get up: the Bible gives many examples of that pattern, such as David and Peter. God does require honesty, though. We dare not misrepresent ourselves to God, for if we do so, we close our hands to grace."[1]

Here's reality: Seeds grow over a long period of time. In the dirt. In the dark. If you dig them up, they cease to grow. And what looks like a weed just may be a plant whose identity you don't yet recognize.

....

Don't close off any part of yourself from Me. I know you inside and out, so do not try to present a "cleaned up" self to Me.

—SARAH YOUNG[2]

Excuse My Language

It's hard to tell parts of my story without swearing. It's not because I swear all the time. I don't. It's just that it's hard to describe—*honestly and accurately*—some horrific and stunning realities of life events in normal, nice words.

Does God care?

Well, of course he does.

Jesus exhorts the Pharisees, "Good people have good things in their hearts, and so they say good things. But evil people have evil in their hearts, so they say evil things" (Matthew 12:35).

Well . . . if I speak of the evil in my child's life as evil—with an evil word—am I bringing up something evil from within evil me or just calling evil evil? D**n that marijuana!

Paul directs us, "When you talk, do not say harmful things, but say what people need—words that will help others become stronger. Then what you say will do good to those who listen to you" (Ephesians 4:29).

So . . . does an unlovely word, uttered from my lips before another who is struggling, tear them down or actually offer them a bridge of understanding and permission to access their own pain and trauma? Life can be so sh***y at times!

If David were writing his psalms to God in the twenty-first century, would he have included a few choice words to express his emotions?

I wonder.

Surely, God cares about my language—how I express my emotions and beliefs in the action of my utterances. I believe he cares that I am careful to honestly and truthfully shape my expression of my trust as well as my doubting confusion. Surely such an effort leads me to mirror God's own expression.

God didn't go all light and fluffy when he sentenced his Son to die a torturous, messy death on a cross. He didn't diminish the pain of the sacrifice. Four-letter word: pain. His Son soul-vented a real experience of abandonment. The descriptions recorded are anything but nice. After Jesus' death, it was dark for three hours. Pitch-black. Dark beyond nice words. Four-letter word: dark.

I don't plan to spend my future cursing like a rapper. But I've found that there are times in my human journey that certain choice words—colorful, four-letter words—emerge to express soul-splitting pain in a way that no other syllables can match. I believe that in such moments, God is listening. I love . . . four-letter word: *love* . . . that.

8

Relinquishment

I'd heard of the hero's journey—where a young man must journey out of the familiar into the shadowy unknown in order to discover himself and send down roots into his future. But when my son took off for parts unknown, first as a preteen and then full on as a young adult, I didn't recognize his departing as that of a budding hero. He looked more like a delinquent to me. Or maybe just lost.

After Ethan's return from out-of-state counseling, for a short while he was better. He finished high school. There were normal moments like homecoming and prom and looking ahead to college. But there were other issues swirling in his world. Girls: Much of Ethan's identity played out with the current girlfriend in his life. It's not that there were lots of girls. There weren't. But when Ethan had a girlfriend, he was seriously attached to her. Like inseparably connected. Like addicted. Alcohol: Ethan didn't just slip a party beer here and there. He downed bottles of vodka or Captain Morgan whiskey. Often. One Christmas Day he was fine in the morning but drunk in the evening. We had no clue where he'd obtained the booze. Sure, we had wine and such around, but he was into more. Addicted. Add to these other struggles: angry outbursts, traffic violations, defiance, legal charges. Ethan was gradually leaving again. The issues amassed until a different kind of help was clearly needed.

I remember walking down the hall in the MOPS office late one afternoon. Everyone had gone home and I was on my own way out.

It was a season of inordinate personal and professional stress. Leading MOPS was more than challenging. And both of my children were making choices with life-and-death consequences.

The weariness weighed on me like concrete. I sighed and mumbled up to heaven, "If I quit MOPS, would the enemy leave my children alone?"

The answer hovered around me, surprising with its clarity: *No.*

Ethan entered an outpatient facility where he followed the steps of AA and stayed sober for a few months. But he fell again. Back into the mix he went until Evan and I held an intervention with his AA sponsor and he agreed to admit himself to inpatient help.

As with our daughter's battle, I revealed Ethan's situation to the board of MOPS International and to our team of leaders. Evan and I leaned hard into faithful friends and family and each other. I shared my anguish with a coworker. She approached me the next day with a vision God had given her: Ethan was surrounded by angels. It was intense, and he was in grave danger. Then the angels drew their swords to protect their charge: Ethan.

The picture gave me hope, and I held it tightly as I prayed and sang my heart out to Matt Redman's "Never Let Go," claiming life for Ethan. *Please, God, please!*

As Ethan completed this treatment, we began to look for the best place for him to go next. He was a young adult by this time—and Evan and I felt strongly that he shouldn't come back home. But where? His sponsor came forward and offered to bring Ethan into his home with his family as a transition step until Ethan was ready for solo living.

Evan and I drove Ethan to the sponsor's home, were warmly greeted, and were shown to the room where Ethan would stay. It was the man's son's room, hastily emptied to make room for Ethan. A twin bed, a dresser, a closet. Just fine. I hugged Ethan and told him how much I loved him, preparing to give once last squeeze. Then I noticed the framed print on the wall above the bed. A young man, surrounded by the wings of a huge angel—holding a spear.

Ethan progressed in that season. He found a job, completed the legal obligations that had hounded him, and steered clear of substance abuse. He moved into a basement apartment next door to his sponsor. For about nine months—I think—he was sober. It was awesome to have him back.

One day I pulled into his driveway to find a strange car at the house. It belonged to a woman he'd met in rehab. A relationship began that brought no good. Addiction returned.

For three to four years the pattern continued: he drank, he made poor choices, the poor choices had deep consequences, he wanted to change, he did for a while, and then he drank again.

This season was *torture*. I'm not trying to be dramatic. Just honest. I have no words but bad ones to describe the pain.

I've always been a Bible reader. I love the Gospels especially. During this time I was reading in Luke, about a chapter a day but sometimes just a paragraph a day. Well, sometimes every other day or just once a week. (Just keeping it real.)

I read Luke 7:12–15, the story of the widow of Nain:

> When he came near the town gate, he saw a funeral. A mother, who was a widow, had lost her only son. A large crowd from the town was with the mother while her son was being

carried out. When the Lord saw her, he felt very sorry for her
and said, "Don't cry." He went up and touched the coffin, and
the people who were carrying it stopped. Jesus said, "Young
man, I tell you, get up!" And the son sat up and began to talk.
Then Jesus gave him back to his mother.

I wondered what kind of death I would have to give Ethan
over to. I reread, "the only son of his mother." I underlined, "Then
Jesus gave him back to his mother."

Give me back my son!

Later I came to Luke 9:38–42, the story of the healing of a boy
with an evil spirit:

> A man in the crowd shouted to him, "Teacher, please come
> and look at my son, because he is my only child. An evil spirit
> seizes my son, and suddenly he screams. It causes him to lose
> control of himself and foam at the mouth. The evil spirit keeps
> on hurting him and almost never leaves him. I begged your
> followers to force the evil spirit out, but they could not do it."
>
> Jesus answered, "You people have no faith, and your lives
> are all wrong. How long must I stay with you and put up with
> you? Bring your son here."
>
> While the boy was coming, the demon threw him on the
> ground and made him lose control of himself. But Jesus gave
> a strong command to the evil spirit and healed the boy and
> gave him back to his father.

I want my son back!

....

One morning the phone rang about two. Evan answered it to find
out Ethan had been arrested. As we prayed and wrestled over

how to respond, we realized that we'd never invested in the lawyer approach with Ethan before. Every parent knows the clear drive to try whatever you can think of to help your child. On the one hand we knew we were close to needing to step back and out of Ethan's life in order to help him. On the other hand, we were driven to not do so until we had exhausted every approach.

The next morning we hired a lawyer to meet Ethan at court, introduce himself, and offer to represent Ethan *if* Ethan would admit himself to the one remaining program available to him: the local rescue mission. It was a yearlong program, free to Ethan—which was essential, as he had neither money nor means of making it at that time—and would be an option for him other than jail. Ethan agreed.

It was December. Evan was traveling for work and it fell to me to collect bail, post it, and then retrieve Ethan. I went to the bank to withdraw the necessary cash, enduring the teller's chirpy, "Wow! Are you off for a Christmas shopping excursion?" I gritted my teeth and replied, "Not today—something far more exciting!" Oh, how I wanted to blurt out, "Nope! I'm actually driving up to the county jail to post bail for my son!" I'd love to have seen the look on her face.

I waited for the court to call and inform me Ethan had been released. The winter night's temperature had fallen to negative 6 degrees. When the call came hours later, I drove to the unfamiliar facility, followed the signs to the correct door, and saw my son in a lightweight hoodie, jeans, and tennis shoes, shivering at the curb. I hadn't seen him in weeks. He looked awful. He had nothing with him. Nothing.

I drove him home in silence. I had no words. Part of me wanted to pull the car over and sob into his cigarette-stinking hoodie. Part of me wanted to kick him out of the car. All of me wanted him *fixed*. Finally, thirty minutes into the drive, my son wept. He'd messed up his life. So bad. So bad.

I still said nothing. I think God just clamped my mouth shut. For me to speak would be to take his feelings. They were his. This was his. He was his.

We pulled into the garage. He was home for the moment. While he showered in his old bathroom, I made soup and laid out some of his father's clothes for him to wear. Warmed at last, I pulled out my Bible and read him both Luke 7 and Luke 9 and told him how very afraid I had been that I would lose him forever—might still. He bent his head and agreed. Jesus gave the son back to his mother.

The next morning Ethan checked into the rescue mission. For the first ninety days—through the Christmas season and then some—he slept in bunk beds with three hundred other homeless people and cleaned up after drunks and street people. That year our Christmas letter showed a photo of Ethan on a snowy city sidewalk, bending down petting his dog, a 104-pound Rottweiler, Darla. We wrote that he'd started a new program to develop and grow himself. It was the truth. What we didn't say is that the picture was taken outside the downtown rescue mission and that Darla was there to visit him with us on Christmas Eve.

There were great shifts in the months that followed. On Father's Day, Ethan had a pass to visit. He was using the bus by now and had called from a pay phone to tell me which stop to meet him at. When I arrived he wasn't there. I wrestled with concern, but there was no way to contact him. Homeless people don't have cell phones.

So I drove home, wondering what had gone wrong. About an hour later the doorbell rang. I opened it to a very sweaty son. Turns out he'd taken another bus and ended up several miles away in another neighborhood. Why was he sweaty? He *ran*. My son *ran* home. He was so excited to see us, to be with his dad on Father's Day, that he ran. Jesus gave the son back to his father.

Wouldn't it be great to end the story with a "happily ever after" of Ethan's graduation a year later and his immediate immersion into a healthy life? I've learned that "happily ever after" isn't always what we get—and actually it may not be God's very best. Ethan didn't graduate from the program. He left just a few weeks shy to return to that same unhealthy relationship where he'd lost himself before.

Having now exhausted all our options—and ourselves—Evan and I finally felt released to step back. It happened much more clearly for Evan than for me. I had thrown myself too heavily into the "happily ever after" posture rather than in the "whatever it takes" one. My husband held me and gently wrenched my heart-fingers from my son. My friends spoke truth to me. I had to face a hard fact: Why would Ethan face his battles if I was fighting them for him? How could he feel his need for God if he had *me?*

Eventually, while the silence and not-knowing wrenched our hearts, an unexplainable peace settled on us. I had a dream where I was beside a community pool. I looked down and saw a baby—a doll—almost like a fetus. It was Ethan. I dove in to get him. I couldn't seem to get a hold to lift him up and out. Then, just as I felt the air gone in my lungs, I felt myself being lifted up to the surface. My arms were empty.

Ethan wasn't a baby. He was a grown man. And it wasn't my job to save him, to bring him back to himself. Can I just say that now I know it can be a *good* thing for parents of adult children to realize that their children are just that: adults? His decisions were his decisions. His consequences were his consequences. His life was his life.

From time to time I attended Al-Anon—the support side of Alcoholics Anonymous for the families and loved ones of addicts. I pored over the materials I'd collected. It helped to know that the two main "weapons" of the addict are anger and anxiety. If they can make you angry at them, they can blame you for their drinking. If they can make you anxious for them, they can make you carry the responsibility and consequences for their actions so they don't have to.

During the peak of Eva's season of struggle a respected leader told me, "Elisa, we are not responsible for our children's choices. We are responsible for our responses to their choices." At that time I worked to put this truth in place. It was time to remember and rehearse this reality with Ethan.

God underlined my lessons as I read August 23 in *Jesus Calling*: "If you let a loved one become an idol in your heart, you endanger that one as well as yourself."[1]

And then one day I'm riding my bike down the trails behind our house. With the air whizzing around me, I feel free. Happy. I sense God saying, *Elisa, get your head up. I have things for you to do.* I know now. I know that I'm finished for now. Maybe there will be other seasons of parenting with Ethan, but for now, I know I need to stop mothering him.

One word describes this completion of my efforts: relinquishment. It has several definitions: to cede (whatever that means), to abandon (no, not that one—*never*), and to let go. Yes. That's it: let go. Let him go.

In her book *An Invisible Thread*, Laura Schroff befriends a homeless boy whom she mentors for a succession of years until, as a young man, he suddenly disappears. She writes of the myth of the hero's journey:

> It is a journey many of us have had to make in one way or another. It happens on our path to discovering who we are and what we are made of. When we are young and full of energy but still naïve about the world, we are lured into a dark, mysterious forest—a forest that seduces us with the promise of great things. There we face challenges more intense than

we could have fathomed, and how we face those challenges determines who we become. If we make it out of the forest alive, we are wiser and stronger, and the gifts we bring back with us will make the world a better place. The hero's journey is a journey of self-discovery.[2]

Six more months pass. Just before Christmas, Ethan calls to see if we can connect. Evan and I take a deep breath. Evan is ready. I'm not. I've just begun to get the hang of this letting go stuff. We talk it over with Eva and our son-in-law, Jason. We all decide to give it a try. Ethan comes for Christmas Eve to spend the night. By the end of the evening he wants to leave his other life. Evan is ready. I am not. I loosen my grip and risk. He stays.

And then he goes again.

We receive a collect call. A request for help. This time there is no rescuing. But we continue to accept the collect calls. I begin to read to him from *Jesus Calling* and the Bible. He asks me to send him the daily readings. I type them out and mail them. They become his manna. He tells us of his discovery of God anew. We pray together. He emerges from the journey broken—and beautiful.

It's been some time since this last going. Ethan is not living with us, but he has not returned to the old. He is on his own, with a new sponsor, a job, and living with sober roommates. He's in school. We see him often and talk with him on the phone more. One weekend I preach in my church and Ethan sits on the front row. The real message in that service doesn't come from my lips. It speaks in the form of a young man, clapping and singing.

His eyes are clear. His smile warms my soul, right-cheek dimple and all. There is a confidence budding forth. When he grabs me in a hug, he brings all of himself to the moment. A friend remarks how deeply his heart is now toward God. He's still not "done." We're not done until we're dead. None of us.

Than. My son. Jesus gave the son back to his mother. And every day I give him back to God. Relinquished.

....

Being broken is both God's work and ours. He brings His pressure to bear, but we have to make the choice ... All day long, the choice will be before us in a thousand ways.

—Roy Hession[3]

Q to the 16th Power

When we begin this parenting journey, we set our sights on the end goal: getting from A to Z. You know, A is birth and the beginning. Z is the end: where your child grows to become a mature-ish, responsible adult who loves God and knows that he has something valuable to contribute to God's kingdom here on earth.

So we step predictably, slowly, and certainly from A to B to C. Potty training. Table manners. Sharing toys with siblings and friends. Family traditions. Simple prayers. Once in a while we're surprised by a seemingly backward movement from C back to B and even A. Like when the doctor says, "Her speech seems to be delayed," or "Let's test him for ADD." Eventually, we learn to take such moments in stride, aware that sometimes we grow forward by stepping back for a bit.

Over the months and years, the linear process continues. Back to C, on to D, then to E. Looking good. Predictable. The way it should be.

For some children and therefore for their parents, an odd turn occurs in this progression toward Z. The child takes a bizarre, unpredicted turn. She moves off the path. He catapults into another dimension. Instead of moving to F, G, H, I, J, K, L . . . , we find our child at Q to the 16th power. Their choices were nowhere in our plans for their lives. Nowhere near our heart's desire. An eating disorder. Failing grades. Rebellion. School behavioral problems. Lying. Depression.

Here's what I'm wondering: if our desire is to move our precious children from A to Z in this quirky world, and if Z is really knowing and loving God no matter what, and if Q to the 16th power gets him or her to Z, then maybe . . . just maybe . . . that's okay.

Does every child go A . . . B . . . C . . . D . . . E . . . F . . . G to Z? Some do. But I didn't. Why do I think my children will? Why do I think my children's friends will? Good questions. And as I ask them, I realize I've come to a crazy conclusion that if I do it "right" as a mom, then my children will move according to the "right" plan. But what's "right"?

Is it more "right" to move A . . . B . . . C . . . D, or is it just as "right" to step through G to Q to the 16th power? I don't know. I only know that if Q to the 16th power gets to Z, then just maybe that's okay— because after all, Z's the goal.

Paul writes in Romans 8:28, "And we know that in all things God works for the good of those who love him, who have been called according to his purpose" (NIV). When our children choose Q to the 16th power, we have a choice as to whether we still believe this truth.

In *all* things, God works for the good of those who love him. X and Y lead to Z. And so does Q to the 16th power.

9

Diversity

Eva walked across the lobby to greet me. In those post-Thomas and pre-Marcus years, we were finding our way back together. She looked lovely in her black-and-white dress. Classy, elegant. Just right for the fund-raiser we were hosting and to which we'd invited her.

And—what else was it about her? She seemed . . . jaunty? As she drew closer, my eyes did a quick scan up and down her put-together outfit. Up and down. And then, just down. Tendrilling up her left leg was a new accessory, one I'd never seen on her body before. Flowers. Vines. A butterfly? Oh . . . a tattoo.

This wasn't just an itsy-bitsy initial or a ladybug or a Scripture verse. This was a garden galloping up my daughter's leg in full bloom. I could practically smell the bouquet!

Oh yippee.

In the shaping season between various events in her life, now-eighteen-year-old Eva had chosen to express her emotions and identity in inked symbols on her body. *Permanent* inked symbols. Can I just say I didn't speak the language? And I wasn't interested in taking the Rosetta Stone course. I remember Evan groaning when he saw it. We were less than prepared for such an expression.

Next came the dragon, the sun, the butterfly, the angel wings, the pair of dice, and the heart. They were followed by the stars, the footprints, and the flower. Oh, and the bird. In recent years there have been special names and birthdates. I noticed a sweet fish not long ago.

My daughter likes her tattoos. They speak a language for her that is both creative and meaningful.

I remember her brother, Ethan, half-joking over Eva's inked expressions. At first. Then a few years later he showed me a picture on his phone—of his first tattoo. From the photo I couldn't make out what it was, or where the image appeared on his body. Kinda concerning. But when I asked, he unbuttoned his shirt and revealed three dog paw prints stamped atop his shoulder: the very place where he had carried home our family dog after she'd been hit and killed by a car. Tears sprang into my eyes.

I began to find my dictionary of meaning for such a gesture.

Since then, he's added his own mural of life-illustrations. Some are still strange to me. Some sacred. Some he'd like to change as he knows he has changed. All say something to him about his life and life lessons.

Diversity is the experience of things that are different from what we know, what we value, and what we expect. And our children teach us diversity big time. So like us and yet so *unlike* us, our children show us they are more than we ever imagined they could be. That they are us and beyond.

Sometimes this is an awe-inspiring reality. My friend Karen Facebooks about her teen football player son: "Favorite moment of Booker's football season? Watching him lead a humble post game prayer for his teammates and his opponents and their families. Hands down, my favorite moment. Love me that Booker boy—a giant among men."

In other moments, not so much. These are more haunting, prophetically concerning, bringing us to our knees to trust yet again.

....

Way back when Eva first began middle school, she ran to the pickup zone clutching a wrinkled envelope in her hand. She opened the car door, threw in her backpack, and plopped in her seat, announcing as she buckled in, "Mom! I've been invited to Stephanie's sleepover!" Her face was alight with joy as she thrust the invitation at me.

"Who's Stephanie?" I asked as I pulled out the card and read the contents. I'd never heard of her.

"Oh, she's a girl in my third-period class. She's cool!"

No help there. And no real help as I read the invitation. I didn't recognize the last name or the address or even the handwriting. Ugh.

"Can I go?" It was the obvious next question. I didn't want to answer it. Actually, I didn't know the answer. I had to think. And research. And talk to Evan.

"We'll see." A mom's automatic response to all things unknown.

I hadn't even begun to adjust to Eva being in middle school. The first day of orientation she'd floored me by carrying down every doll and every piece of doll paraphernalia she owned from her upstairs room and placing it in a heap by our back door, announcing, "I don't need this stuff anymore."

What? The Cabbage Patch Doll I'd carefully selected and then Eva had "adopted" on her sixth Christmas? The little cradle that went with it? The high chair? "Well, you never know, Eva. You might want them for your children." Right.

"I'm done with them, Mom," she responded.

Should have been a clear enough clue for the day a few weeks later when Stephanie suddenly became my daughter's newest interest.

Not only was I not ready for Eva to leave her childhood behind, I wasn't ready for her to spread her wings out of our tight and happy neighborhood into other subdivisions. Middle school opened access to families who lived farther north, east, west, and south of us. People I didn't know living on streets I didn't drive through on my normal errands.

I decided to call Stephanie's mother and "interview" her to see if I thought it would be appropriate for Eva to attend the sleepover. When the phone picked up, there was a very young voice on the other end, too young to even be Stephanie, I thought. "Oh, my mom's asleep," the little sister replied. At four thirty on a school day? She must be on drugs, I decided. Or sells them. No way was Eva going. (Yes, of course I realize now that I was assuming Stephanie's mom was like my mom had been. That Eva would go to Stephanie's and smoke cigarettes and do all kinds of naughty things while Stephanie's mom was "out of it.")

Evan thought differently. He thought I was making way too much of things. "Besides," he reminded me, "you'll be out of town that weekend. I'll take care of it."

My throat clenched. Oh yeah, I was speaking that weekend. If I was out of town, I wouldn't even be able to drive Eva to and from—and to check things out for myself.

As I prepped for the speaking engagement, I loaded up my makeup bag. I'd been so distracted by Eva's ordeal that I'd not spent much time preparing my talks. I figured I'd make up for any possible lack of depth by looking good. A song was going through my head: *"He who began a good work in you . . ."* I hummed along. Then the song went from the back of my mind to the front of my mind as it finished the words of Philippians 1:6 (NIV), *"I'll be faithful to complete it in Eva."*

God was the one who began the good work in Eva, and he would be the one to complete the good work in Eva. While it made good sense that I would worry over Stephanie's slumber party and whether or not Eva should set foot in her house, my *worrying* over it would do nothing but distract *me* from trusting him.

Eva went to the sleepover. She didn't smoke. She didn't end up caring about Stephanie all that much. Now I know that while my concerns had merit—mothers very much need to know where their daughters are going and what they are doing there—mine were rooted in fear. Fear of things I didn't know, didn't like, didn't understand, didn't comprehend how God could use.

Oh, how much I had to learn on this topic! And mercy, how much our children have to teach us! Way back at the baby shower that my friend Cindy gave me for Eva, she shared the words that our children can either be our trophies—sitting on the mantelpieces of our lives and proclaiming how very effective and successful we are as their parents—or they can become our teachers, instructing us about our world, our families, and ourselves.

My friend Amy returns from a holy meeting with her adult daughter, a daughter she has strained to know and understand over the years. Amy whispers a prayer in my presence, "Oh Lord, teach me about my daughter who is so *different* from me. Help me to learn from her and to love her the way she needs me to love her." I sit back in my chair and receive her words into my own mother-child relationships.

We do life so differently. All of us. As we yield to God completing *his* good work in us. Young and old. This generation and the one above it and the one below it and the one below that. Each generation chooses its own language of value—and rebellion. Each of us considers our view the "right" view, even the "biblical" perspective, and then we urge others to adopt our view as their own. When they don't, we scratch our heads in surprise. Or throw darts of judgment in frustration.

Doug Pitt, brother of famous actor Brad Pitt, remarked on *The Today Show* about his upbringing and his life today, "Moms and dads and kids disagree all over the world . . . we can learn from each other."[1]

I remember sitting on the soft couch in a counselor's office worrying about my grandson, Marcus. He'd been at our house the night before, and in a moment, I found him squatting on the floor, working his fingers. His thinking was visible as he silently gestured: one, two, three, four, five—and then on to the next hand: six, seven—clearly counting. With his face all crinkled, he looked up, "Yia Yia, how many grandparents do I have?"

"Eight." We reviewed them together. Then I added my triumphal, "But you only have *one* BeePeez and *one* Yia Yia." To which he smiled, nodded, and agreed. Oh, how I love those tie-it-up-in-a-bow moments!

But I worried. I asked my counselor, "How will he sort through all the relationships in his life?"

She replied, "Elisa, this is *Marcus's* story. It's *his* story that is shaping him. Just as *your* story has shaped you."

When the traditional Christian radio station in Denver was purchased by a ministry airing more contemporary fare, several of my older friends bemoaned the loss of their favorite hymn channel. "Why did they change it?" I heard.

To offer a choice that younger generations might actually listen to?

We don't like change when it's in a direction that makes us uncomfortable. When it's new. When it's different. When it's not what we're used to.

....

Diversity births from the unexpected—both tragic and delightful. Each generation—from builders to boomers, and then from boomers to busters to Xers to millennials and on to edgers, or whatever they end up being called—births a new version of people on this planet. Along with the people come the choices they make: Divorce. Adoption. Disability. Addiction. Fame. Genius. Beauty. Diversity results when we recognize—and learn to welcome—what is unfamiliar into the family.

Brenda didn't expect to raise a special-needs child. But when her son, Zach, was accidentally dropped on his head and sustained a traumatic brain injury, Brenda opened her arms to a world she never imagined.[2]

Marilyn never dreamed she'd become a widow at age fifty. But when her husband died from pancreatic cancer, Marilyn joined the ranks of a "club" she never wanted even to visit.

At sixty-something, Myra learned that her son and his wife would be divorcing after nearly two decades of marriage. She couldn't imagine her large family enduring the fracture, much less moving through and beyond it. The holidays loomed, and she prayed over how to prepare. It seemed her usual wide-armed and lavish love would land in the empty places left by the choices of those around her. Now she struggled over just who to invite to the table. Of course her son. But her former daughter-in-law? His new girlfriend? What a mess!

In church one Sunday she bowed her head and her heart and felt God leading as she sensed him saying, "Extend your table."

The result was questionable, but her action was obedient. "You're always on solid ground when you obey—regardless of the outcome," Myra tells me.

Such differences—such variety—such *diversity* threads through the tapestry of our families and, for that matter, through our entire globe, creating dimension, depth, and an extravagant expression of the God who weaves. We are wise to learn to embrace and even enjoy the multifaceted reality about us. As Croatian theologian Miroslav Volf prophesies, "It may not be too much to claim that the future of our world will depend on how we deal with identity and difference."[3]

Our concept of a life lived for God can—in the end—be oh so different from his. Our God is, himself, diverse, and he embraces a diverse people. He speaks all languages. He glorifies himself through myriad styles of music. He dwells in every country. Every life is special to him. Things we have no room for, he not only embraces but redeems because he can see in, through, and in spite of.

In some ways my children—in their diverse lives—will always be outside of my comfort zone. But that doesn't mean they are outside of God's economy. Brennan Manning writes, "While we love someone for what we find in him or her . . . Jesus loves men and women not for what he finds in them, but for what he finds in himself."[4]

God promises to complete the good work he began in *each* man and woman he creates.

Read those last two paragraphs again if you need to. I did.

....

Everybody is a genius. But if you judge a fish by its ability to climb a tree, it will live its whole life believing it is stupid.

—Attributed to Albert Einstein

Grand*one*

Marcus and Eva lived with us for the first two and a half years of his life. Upstairs. In the very rooms I had dreamed they would inhabit.

We grew to love the shared space, hearing the pats on the hall door that meant Marcus was up and ready to greet the day—and us. Then came the every-morning ritual of chocolate chip waffles, watching BeePeez shave, helping Mama get ready.

Eventually, Eva met and married Jason, and the inevitable occurred: she and Marcus moved out to begin their lives with him. And then there was Marcus's birthfather, who also wanted a share of the parenting action.

I grieved. It felt like loss. A hole in my soul appeared yet again. My heart shrank and shriveled in expectation of the change and then with the reality of it. I worried over all Marcus would be juggling. About his leaving his familiar life in his home that had been our home.

A friend recast the arrangement for me. "Elisa, Marcus isn't *losing* anything. He's gaining. This is about the *more* that God is bringing into his life."

Months later Marcus and I sat at our kitchen table. It was a Marcus and Yia Yia night. I asked Marcus to pray over his Chicken Goldfish Soup. He said, "It's your turn, Yia Yia." I said, "No, you can pray." And he did. Obediently.

When he looked up, I said, "You don't know who Jesus is, do you?"

He said, "Nope."

"Well, Jesus is God," I said.

"Really?" he asked, surprised.

So I explained: Mary and Joseph had a baby named Jesus. He was actually God's Son and Joseph was more like his adopted dad. (Hard stuff here.) We celebrate his birthday with Christmas. Jesus grew up to be a man and a carpenter—he made things with wood like tables and chairs. Then when he was older, he died on the cross so that we could live forever with God.

Even with all of his three and a half years applied, Marcus didn't get this, so I moved on.

"Jesus wants to come and live in our hearts so that when we need help to obey Mommy and Daddy, he can help us. Jesus loves you, Marcus."

"He does?"

"Yes."

"That's amazing!"

"Do you want to ask Jesus to live in your heart?"

"Not now, Yia Yia. It's full right now. I'm eating and my soup is in there."

My heart smiled. I thought about how God had already enlarged it to embrace Marcus's extended world.

And I glimpsed the beginnings of Marcus's own enlarging heart. To embrace his daddy. His new home. His birthfather. His *story*. And one day, I prayed, his Savior.

10

Partnership

The night sixteen-year-old Eva's pregnancy test was positive, Evan was traveling for work. While I don't recommend telling your husband that his teenage daughter is pregnant over the phone—*ever*—I couldn't keep the news to myself. I remember his stunned silence, breathing in and out. Then his cracked voice. And my stable husband spilled out. As if my heart wasn't broken already, it split yet again at the sound of his grief.

But let me back up. You don't yet fully know Evan, my husband and my partner in all things parenting. I met him in a rather unexpected season when I'd pretty much given up on finding my life mate.

I remember that morning beginning like every day: me tugging at the aqua quilt, centering its diamond pattern on the double bed. My grandmother, Munna, had made it for me as a high school graduation present, and it had accompanied me wherever I'd studied ever since. Now twenty-three years old, in seminary and living in an extra bedroom of a married student's home, I chewed over my life circumstances and spit out prayers to God as I made my bed.

Lately I'd been fed up with dating and the exhaustion of it all. My prayers that day were no surprise to God as I regularly speed-dialed him on the subject. When he actually responded that morning, I wasn't sure what to make of his words. Maybe it was a bad connection?

Separate thyself unto Me, I heard. Kinda archaic language, I thought. But the phrase kept repeating, over and over, until an image coincided with it: a beautiful black horse pulling a covered carriage and equipped with blinders around its eyes. Like you might see in a Dickensian picturescape of London. With the blinders employed, a horse could only see straight ahead—neither to the right or the left. Unless the driver turned its head in a specific direction.

Separate thyself unto Me. A figure of me—with blinders—appeared in my mind.

Hm.

To be honest, I was grateful for the reprieve. After my first year of seminary in Colorado, far away from every single male I knew from home, I'd grown weary of the mate-seeking process. Sure, I longed to be married as much as I yearned to know how I would provide for myself through ministry—and in what role I'd end up. But nobody I'd dated seemed to float my boat, if you know what I mean. So I journaled God's words and tried to focus in on the directive in my days.

A few months went by and a new semester began. Weeks into it, I raced into Old Testament class and snagged the only empty seat in sight. The professor had already begun the lecture, but my mind was on my next class, where I was required to translate a scripture from Greek to English in a pop quiz format. I hadn't even peeked at the assignment, and it was time to multitask.

"Are you a second-year student?" The question came from

the guy next to me, where I had plunked down and started rummaging through my backpack.

"Yeah." One word. That ought to deter him.

"Are you an MDiv?" he asked, referring to the Master of Divinity track.

"Yeah." We were up to two words now. I wondered how many it would take before he gave up. I found my Greek New Testament and straightened up in my seat, searching for the required passage.

"How are you liking Greek?" Really. All this while our professor was lecturing on and I was in a panic about the pop quiz now just forty-five minutes away. Sighing, I turned my head, all ready to clip off the conversation for good.

Bam! Our eyes met. I took in a breath and stared. I have no idea what we said next. I just remember a clear image: the driver turning the head of the horse.

Evan Morgan and I married just months later. Our courtship was clear and quick. Just weeks after that initial head-turning moment, I asked God, "Is he the one?" And I knew. I just knew.

How? Well, there was this *fit*. My personality was up and down and excited and exhausted. (Evan has always said I have two speeds: on and off.) In comparison, Evan was so . . . *stable*. Raised in a Christian home with Christian parents, he looked like Billy Graham compared to my splotchy past. He was a business major first settling into banking, and then migrating from his native Laramie, Wyoming, down to Denver Seminary to resolve a nagging nudge that he should pursue ministry. After a year of classes, and in our first year of marriage, he returned to banking only to be recalled to the same seminary as the CFO. Our crazy and creative God had put him where he needed to be, using a dot-to-dot matrix of leading. Evan was handsome, humble, loving, and deeply committed to God, and he was unafraid— though also somewhat naive—of my rugged upbringing.

God fit us together.

There was also a kind of *call* to each other. When on our second "date" (a run to Burger King to fetch a Whopper) he revealed that he'd had cancer just a few years prior and as a result wouldn't be able to father children, an alarm went off in me. Not the negative kind. More like metal to a magnet. And not because I didn't want to have children. It's just that there was this core *call* to connect with him. And I think him to me. A need-to-need attraction. So in addition to *fit*, there was this *call*. A call to completion?

Knowing that we wanted children but that we would wait *long* for them due to the waiting lists in our state, we applied to adopt early in our marriage. In that first season our days, nights, and weekends swirled with friends and ministry and family. We were filled to full with life. I worked at the college, he at the seminary, and we both served with the singles at church. Evan pursued his real estate and then financial planning credentials to cover the enormous cost of adoption that was well beyond our ministerial salaries.

Eventually our endurance tanks began to run low—was there a leak somewhere?—and the reality of our childlessness drew even more from our reserves. Four and a half years into our life together we were approved but still waiting for a baby. I remember just shutting the door to the already prepared nursery. I'd thunk the mattress and dust would fly. It was too painful to see it empty.

At last, our daughter arrived. That first night she slept on Evan's chest, her fingers curled tight, grasping the cotton of his T-shirt. He rode her on his shoulders in and out of those toddler years. When Ethan appeared, Evan's love multiplied.

Evan was—and still is—a tremendous dad. Up at 4:30 a.m. to take a Greek class to complete his own seminary training, he took the first shift with baby Eva. He alternated with me over baths and bedtime, counting the ladybugs in Kenneth Taylor's

Jesus books. He timed at swim meets, threw the ball to Ethan, accompanied Eva on dad/daughter dates, and forayed in the wild to catch fish and mice and whatever else Ethan was in the mood to capture.

In the early years of our children's lives, I was home with them, hiring a nanny a few hours a week to cover while I wrote or spoke. When God called me to lead MOPS International, Evan was the first to prompt me to accept. He'd arrive at church some Sunday mornings, our kids in tow, and the pastor would chuckle and ask, "Is Elisa traveling?" as he eyed the cockeyed placement of Eva's hair bow. "Hey," Evan shrugged, "I got the bow in, didn't I?"

We took turns in that era. I'd leave before dawn to be at my desk by six while Evan got the kids off to school. On the drive, he'd dial my office and I'd pray into the ears of my little ones for their day. Then I'd handle school pickup and homework until he returned for dinner. We were partners in parenting, and it worked well for us.

Oh, sure, there were bumps. Ours wasn't a traditional setup for a Christian family. In private there were moments when Evan chafed against my public platform and the hiddenness of his role in my life, saying he felt like a professional golfer's spouse, walking hole to hole and clapping and cheering at my shots.

Yet, when asked, Evan was always my greatest fan. More than once he's been asked how he copes with having a public leader like me for a wife. His answer still oozes warm comfort through me: "One day I know I'm going to stand before God and give account for how I've used the gifts he's entrusted to me. And I want to say I have used them well. But I think he'll also ask me how I've supported my wife in using hers. It's my job to lift up her gifts. All of them."

As much as we shared and traded off and on, beneath the surface, I can see now that in the beginning years, I assumed most of the responsibility for raising our children. Maybe a better word is *pre*sumed. I was the *mom*. Because our kids were adopted and I hadn't carried them in pregnancy, I felt I had to somehow make up for that loss and so felt compelled to do all the feeding myself—to bond with them and them with me. When I grew impatient with a baby who wouldn't go back to sleep in the middle of the night, it was hard for me to ask Evan for help. I was raised (sort of) by a single mom. I didn't have the role model of a dad. As much as I longed for the happily-ever-after life of having both a mom and dad for our kids, I thought I should be able to handle the everyday elements of parenting on my own.

To me, the mom was the manager of the family. The dad was security, a playmate, and a provider. All these were things I missed out on as a child, and therefore in some crazy way, I saw a dad as an accessory. A necessary accessory—and one I desperately wanted my children to enjoy—but not *essential* to survival.

When Evan and I disagreed on our parenting approaches, I came up with lists of reasons that I was right. I'd been in the parenting role so long! Forever it seemed. Add to my personal trauma survival the fact that I'd been trained as a counselor and, well, surely I knew best!

Over time, Evan learned to challenge me, standing toe to toe to make his parental opinions known. It was new territory for me—listening and letting him have a say. Sometimes.

We were both growing up, Evan and I. While I was slogging through my need to prevent the breakage of my first family in my second family, Evan began to peel the veneer off some of the expectations he'd inherited from his first family: Christians don't make mistakes. They don't rebel. They are good people who do good things with good results. If you're following God, you go to church, you don't cuss, and your marriage and your kids look good to others.

Uh-oh.

To be fair, such expectations had pretty much always been met in Evan's experience. He'd received his faith in God with his oatmeal, as predictable as the passage of the hours on the clock. His parents cookie-cuttered each day with a routine that rarely varied, his dad as dean of engineering at the university, his mom as a happy housewife, his two older brothers growing up sharing a room all together with him in their two-bedroom house. Until Evan faced and conquered cancer, there had been little to ruffle the smooth waters of his small-town sea. And even with cancer, he felt God reassured him of his future as a dad when in the recovery room, he whispered to the nurse, "There must be a special baby out there for me to adopt."

As he matured as a man, a husband, and a father, he began to evaluate his own upbringing, and as we all do, he discovered some holes even in his happily knit family. While well versed in the Bible and theology, Evan's father rarely attended his sporting events and had no idea how to initiate a father/son conversation of significance. His temper had a quick draw. Evan's mom—an amazingly loving saint to the entire town of Laramie, Wyoming—worried her way through every car ride, vacation, and emerging medical symptom.

Young adulthood is a season of evaluation and *re*evaluation: of what we thought was normal in our families of origin as well as what we believe we are to carry forward in our families of creation. Just as I was working hard to be the mother I never had, Evan was shaping his husbandly and fatherly offering in response to the parenting he had received. The thing is that my need to direct traffic, so to speak, often stalled his efforts at a red light.

Then when we discovered Eva was pregnant, for a long while I refused to let the light turn green.

....

When we learned sixteen-year-old Eva was pregnant, I took over. I assumed command. It's what I did. I found a doctor for Eva. I went with her to the appointments. While I'd never been pregnant, I'd surely been to OB/GYNs. I knew enough of the drill, or certainly more than Evan knew. I helped her research teen pregnancy centers. I set up family counseling sessions. Evan participated. He attended every discussion to which he was invited. But I remained Admiral of All. I sat on the couch with my daughter and played cards and watched reality TV, creating an island where Eva and I marooned ourselves from others. Lashed about us like a life raft was the stunning reality of what we were facing. It was *we* who were facing it, but I absorbed as much of the responsibility as I could. I thought I was helping. Evan retreated to our bedroom and watched golf. He thought he was helping.

When Thomas came into the world prematurely, my attention-giving efforts couldn't stretch to match the multiplied needs. I couldn't go with Thomas and be with Eva—and I had to stay with Eva. Evan, clearly *called* to the moment, arose and shepherded our tiny grandson across town to the neonatal unit. Alone with a baby stuck and stabbed with tubes and machines, Evan cried out to God to help Thomas *know* he was not alone. That he was wanted and loved. Thomas clutched Evan's outstretched finger in response.

When I returned from Eva duty late that night, Evan told me he couldn't wait to develop the photo of that moment that he'd snapped on the disposable camera he'd grabbed in the hospital gift shop. Evan had picked up that baby with his very heart and was committed to carrying him forward until God provided permanent parents. At the relinquishment ceremony, other than Eva, Evan was the most visibly ripped apart in the releasing of Thomas, even though he knew God had called forth exactly the right parents for that precious child.

The reality of not being able to be present for Thomas when I had to be present with Eva revealed to me a need I could no longer deny: I couldn't parent alone. I'd peeked at this truth before in my parenting efforts—when a child wouldn't *ever* sleep through the night or use the potty, or struggled to remember spelling words revealing a learning disorder, or belligerently stayed out later than curfew. I'd surely seen Evan involve himself and command good results. I knew he was a great dad and more than capable of being a fabulous parent. But in this crisis of all things family, I innately depended *first and foremost* on myself. The very real presence of my grandson, in a hospital separate from my daughter, tore my solo act apart for good. For my good. For Evan's good. For the good of our family.

We are not meant to parent alone. None of us. Yes, many of us do parent alone—we find ourselves solo because there is no partner. Maybe we've been left, or we left another. Maybe our partner has passed away. Maybe there really never was anyone but us. But this is not what God intended. He meant for children to have two parents, two people who can spell each other and balance each other and talk each other down from cliffs and out of ridiculous corners.

My mothering was heartfelt, tenacious, and all-out. I did much good with my commitment to my children and intuitively responded to their needs in ways that made huge differences for their futures. But for much of my marriage, I disallowed myself the help I could have in my husband and a partner in parenting. Yes, we traded off parenting chores fairly enough. I'd fought for and won a generous equality of shared investment. But the soulful carrying of my children I saw as solo. I'd separated myself unto . . . what? Unto God? Or unto myself and what made sense to me?

Maybe it seemed to me that Evan didn't know what to do in a crisis the way I knew what to do from so many layers of personal experience. But he would learn—by immersing himself in the struggle. Just as I had.

In the thick of the hard times with our children, one particular night formed my husband's faith in a way that has carried him forward as a father. He couldn't sleep, and so as was his custom, he rose to pace about our house, taking the loop: family room to kitchen to dining room to living room to entryway, and back to family room. Lap after lap, calling out to God, questioning and angry. He'd tried to be a good husband and a faithful father, to live his life in obedience and with integrity. Now there was this *mess* that was our family—with no resolution or redemption in sight.

Maybe it's best if I share this story in Evan's own words:

Finally I just sat down in the bay window of our breakfast room and looked up at the sky. Honestly, I'd *had* it. But I felt *compelled* to look at the stars. I'd always been intrigued by the galaxies. And in that moment, one of my favorite psalms filtered through my thoughts: "When I consider your heavens, the work of your fingers, the moon and the stars, which you have set in place, what is mankind that you are mindful of them?" (Psalm 8:3–4 NIV).

It was like God was drawing my gaze upward—to consider his heavens. I couldn't *not* look. Yet I couldn't figure out what was going on, what I was supposed to see or understand.

"Yeah. Yeah. I know, you're all-powerful and all," I said sarcastically through the glass of the window up to the sky. I couldn't believe I was acting this way toward God and I half expected him to zap me in the moment. But I was just so sick of it all. In this weary night watch I relented: "I see it all, God. You made all this. You're infinite. *Whatever!*"

Still, I couldn't take my eyes off the night sky. And then Orion's Belt came into focus. My eyes were nailed to it. I couldn't pull them away. Astronomy wasn't even a hobby for me, but everything I'd ever known about that constellation whirled through my mind. Orion's Belt: three stars, seemingly perfectly aligned and yet most likely hundreds of millions of miles apart from each other. For some reason I imagined myself in an airplane—no, a spaceship circling in the cosmos, and then around a single star in the formation. I realized that from that vantage point—going around just one of the three stars—I couldn't really see or even know about the other stars, much less how they aligned together to make a unique constellation.

And then I heard God speak to me—as in no other moment in my life. I'll never forget it. *Evan, from where I sit, it all lines up.* Suddenly I was sitting with God, next to him in his celestial seat, viewing eternity past and future, without limitations. God laid his hand on my shoulder, and pointed out the stars to me: a picture of his providence and sovereignty in our lives. From no other place could I have comprehended . . . from where he sits, *it all lines up.*

Evan grandparented Thomas with a greater presence than I could offer. And he parented our children with efforts I'd thought only I could provide. When Eva had the accident, it was Evan who first received the call and rushed to the hospital while I was states and hours away. When she turned from the abusive relationship, it was Evan who whisked Eva to a treatment center. Evan brought Ethan home from residential rehab. And Evan bowed his head one Christmas Eve and determined that we should agree to Ethan's request to return home that last time when I could not bring myself to welcome him.

In her book *An Unfinished Marriage,* author Joan Anderson tells the story of the rebirth of her thirty-something-year marriage. I see my own lessons in her self-observation: "I've come to know that I can have power or love—but not both."[1] Power can surely protect us. But it can also insulate us unnecessarily.

Fear, pride, and self-defense can keep us from the partnership God provides for us. Just as it kept me from allowing God himself to love me, my need to do life right—myself and by myself—separated me from the help God had prepared for me in my husband.

I know full well that Evan needed me as much as I needed him. That is clear. I brought strengths and skills to our parenting that he did not yet possess. But in my needing to be needed—and my refusal to have needs myself—what did I miss?

Well into our kids' teenage years, but before the brokenness in our family revealed itself, Evan and I committed to go to counseling together. Our goal was to prepare ourselves for the empty-nest years. To make sure our marriage was ready to narrow down to just us again. Instead, when our lives broke apart around us in that season, we focused on just keeping one nostril out of the water and treading to stay alive. Our marriage was changed in ways we never expected yet deeply needed.

Each session began with the therapist asking, "How are you, Elisa? How are you, Evan? How's your marriage?" The first two questions were easy enough, but the question about our marriage was new. And challenging. And refreshing. And paradigm-shifting. How *was* our marriage? As if it were an entity all its own, a *being*, Evan and I turned toward each other with question marks on our faces. Slowly, we began to examine the living, breathing reality of our marriage, to learn from it, to respect it, to count its fingers and toes and watch its wobbly steps and major milestones, and eventually, to *cherish* it for something wholly different from us individually.

Paul writes in 1 Corinthians 11:11–12 words that jump from the page at me: "Nevertheless in the Lord woman is not independent of man, nor is man independent of woman. For as woman came from man, so also man is born of woman. But everything comes from God" (NIV). Surely this is a gnarly passage often used to address issues of gender propriety in worship. But it's also a powerful comment on the interdependence of man and woman—of husband and wife—of father and mother. We are not independent of each other. Just as God expressed his image in two genders through creation of man and woman, so he calls us together to procreate—and to parent.

Scripture makes clear that his perfect desire for parenting is marriage, that every child might have a mother and a father. In our broken, messy world, we are often left with less than perfect on this planet. Partnership in parenting can come in sharing the load with grandparents, with siblings, with friends and neighbors and the body of Christ represented in the church community. Sometimes help comes even in the legacy we've been left from the lives of those who have passed before us into eternity. The point is that we recognize that we need more than "me" and that we receive the partnership God provides: first in himself and then in the others he brings around us.

Not long ago my brother remarked on how I've changed when I talk about Evan. Since he's known us forever, I was intrigued and asked what he meant. "It used to be that you talked about Evan from a distance. Now, when you speak of him, he is the river in the terrain of your life." The river. The source. The place I go to for sustenance and perspective. For help. The comment hits home. I sense that there's truth here. Odd that I hadn't noticed this for myself. But then we often can't make out the shifts in our own development until they are pointed out to us.

For me, partnership in parenting means recognizing and receiving the man God has named my husband and the father of my children. By God's sovereign hand, Evan has been where I could not be. I've watched him invest. My trust has enlarged. My heart has lightened, as has my load.

From where God sits, it all lines up.

....

You can survive on your own. You can grow strong on your own. You can even prevail on your own. But you cannot become human on your own.

—FREDERICK BUECHNER[2]

Different

Evan and I differ in how we parent our children. Even our play habits revealed a contrast. When they were little, I cooed. I built blanket forts and dragged armloads of books inside, where we read and giggled. Evan's style was to walk in the door, grab our toddler, and throw her up in the air with a "Whoop!"

Differences in parenting styles can be cause for conflict. Many times I've bristled with Evan's choices. He lets the kids go down the street to play when I haven't yet met *that* family (I haven't approved their eligibility to interact with *my* children). He sees nothing wrong with buying a trampoline for the backyard (yikes—lawsuit material!) and a puppy (just another baby in my book) for the family.

His choices are often not *my* choices. They bug me. And when I get bugged . . . well, I tend to criticize. I can become downright mean.

It starts like this: We're all at dinner and the subject of a trampoline comes up. "Puh-leeeeeeze, Mom? *Dad* says it's okay!" I look at Evan. We've had *many* conversations on this subject. He thinks trampolines are fun. I imagine my neck craned from every window in the house to the backyard, and an ambulance and stretcher in waiting.

"When did you say it was *okay*?" I hiss. He can't miss the glare in my eyes, nor can he ignore my leg now wrapped around his ankle in a vice grip under the table.

It's in moments like these that I conclude all logical and rational powers have evaporated from my dear husband's brain. In their place I see "irresponsible" and "immature." And because that's what I think I see, my actions are less than respectful.

May the God who gives endurance and encouragement give you a spirit of unity among yourselves as you follow Christ Jesus, so that with one heart and mouth you may glorify the God and Father of our Lord Jesus Christ. (Romans 15:5–6 NIV)

These words from Paul come from a passage on differences and on how to make room for them rather than judge them. Oops. No unity with us. Instead, it's me versus him, my right way against his obviously wrong one. Oh yeah, and a few confused kids.

Over the years, Evan and I have had many differences of opinion on the subject of how to parent our children. But what we have in common is the end goal: that they grow up to be God-loving people in the process of becoming like Jesus. What I'm learning to embrace is the reality that when the goal is common, the governance of it in the daily-ness of life can differ. There's room for *his* way and *my* way. In fact, our children need both ways.

And so . . . I gave in. We got a trampoline.

The kids are thrilled. Evan gloats. And I'm stretching my neck muscles—and my character—in amazing new directions.

II

Faith

I cradled my much-needed coffee and chatted with Shayne as we prepared to board flights taking us in different directions but to the same destination: home. We'd been in Washington, D.C., for a ONE Mom brainstorming meeting, sponsored by the ONE campaign (one.org). After hearing from some of the world's experts about global health developments and being prepped for our upcoming site visit to Kenya, we ONE Moms had debriefed till the wee hours. It was hard to get up for our 6:00 a.m. cab to the airport.

We grabbed a quick breakfast—my yogurt exploded, and I dodged its contents. A crazy moment. And then, just as my flight was announced, my phone rang. Shayne paused while I answered, my face falling from amusement with my breakfast mess to shock. As she took in the shift in my expression, her face knotted with concern.

On the other end I could hear wailing in the background. Eva? My son-in-law, Jason, said clearly, "Eva's water just broke." *What?!*

The wailing continued as I wrestled sense into my thoughts. "When?"

"Just now."

"Did you call the doctor?"

"No—Eva said to call you."

Well, of course she did. "Call the doctor, Jason. Right now."

"There was a lot of fluid. It's too early," he responded.

She was just twenty-two weeks along. "I know. Call the doctor. I'll call Dad and ask him to get Marcus to school. Call me back after you talk to the doctor."

I punched off Jason and speed-dialed Evan. He answered and I explained. Here we were again: crisis. We prayed together. Jason called back. The doctor said to go to the hospital.

Right. "Evan will meet you there and take care of Marcus. Just go. *Now.*"

On the other end of the call, Jason handed the phone to Eva. I was supposed to calm her down while he threw things together.

Eva wailed in my ear and I prayed in hers. My plane continued boarding. I waved good-bye to Shayne, mouthing, *Please pray!* It was a nearly four-hour flight home to Denver. As I boarded I texted three people: my pastor; my dear friend Carol, Eva's godmother, asking her to go to the hospital; and Karen, a friend who'd lost a baby just one hour after he was born ten years before. Karen and I had been close ever since her devastation, and she came immediately to mind in this moment. I texted her, begging her to pray. The plane door closed, and I sat in my middle bulkhead seat for four hours, vacillating between prayer, panic, and a surreal peace.

Surely this baby would make it, I decided. After all, Thomas had survived and thrived at twenty-seven weeks in utero. This wasn't that far off, was it? Thomas was now *nine years old* and completely fine. I fully expected to land and discover that the doctor had performed an emergency C-section and that Eva's baby would be born.

When the plane touched down I slid my phone on, called

Evan and listened in confusion as he told me they were all with the doctor now. There was very little amniotic fluid left. It wasn't looking good. He handed the phone to Eva. She said, "Please hurry, Mom."

I tried to prepare myself for what was ahead as I hurtled down the highway, but how do you do that—really? I imagined being strong. I pictured hard decisions. I envisioned God miraculously intervening. When I rushed into that hospital room filled with Eva and Jason and Evan and Carol, I looked from one face to another and took in fear—no, despair.

The doctor arrived with the results of Eva's blood work. At the moment she was stable, but infection was likely. The options before Eva and Jason were to try to keep the baby inside, even though the fluid was minimal, or induce labor. If she developed an infection, Eva would be in danger. Either way, the baby would not survive.

What? He was twenty-two weeks! We'd just found out he was a he! The news just did not compute to me. Nor to any of us. We'd been through Thomas. The doctor seemed ignorant. What did she know? I did not like her. She seemed cold and uncaring. Finally a neonatal nurse sat down with us, and somehow her words penetrated our shock and registered. After she left, Eva's next round of blood work showed she was developing an infection. We all left the room to give Eva and Jason time to talk.

Months earlier, Eva had called me to chat, and in the conversation she said, "Mom, Jason and I are trying to get pregnant." You'd have thought I'd be happy, right? I teetered. Marcus was now five and doing great. Eva and Jason had been married several years. It was time. But I was scared. Of what? I'm not sure ... but as I hesitated, she announced clearly, "Mom, if you're not going to be excited about this, then I'm not going to talk with you about it."

I plunged into embracing their decision. A few months later

they called to tell Evan and me that they were expecting. Woo hoo! Marcus wore a "Big Brother" T-shirt, and they told their friends. Eva downloaded the baby growth app on her phone, and we watched the little dot grow every week. Jason moved the office furniture to the basement, and they bought nursery furniture at a garage sale. Good times!

Until that March day when a baby settled still in my daughter's dry womb. *Their* baby. Marcus's brother. My next grandson.

Being a child of an alcoholic trains you for the next crisis—and the next. Add to that my training for hospital chaplaincy and counseling and CEO-ing, and all the potholes we'd already encountered as a family, and let's just say, I went into mom/master/manager role. They had so much to face. Between being pregnant and losing a son came *delivering* a baby. Eva had only had C-sections before. She'd had zero prep. Nor had Jason. Nor had I.

Back in the room, as the doctor explained the procedure for the baby's delivery, Eva teared up and Jason rested his hand on her shaking shoulder. While her baby was still alive at the moment, she would bring forth a baby who would likely already have passed from this life.

Jason looked at me and asked me to stay with them. Eva nodded. "You've been there the other two times. You should be here now."

Over the next few hours nurses came and went, offering comfort but little hope. Carefully, they opened conversations about what the parents wanted: Would they hold him? Would they name him? Pictures? A funeral? Evan and I left the room again for Eva and Jason to process. When we returned it was decided: Eva would hold the baby. They would not name him. They did not want pictures. There would be no funeral.

I had my opinions—strong ones. Of course they should hold him! And name him! I'd been praying all day that they would name him Malachi. That was Eva's runner-up name for Marcus.

And yes, they should have pictures! But I closed my lips and nodded to their decisions, knowing these were their choices, not mine.

Evan had gone to care for Marcus. Ethan had bussed across town to be present. The two of us with Jason sat vigil as Eva's labor began. There were hours to go.

Two lifelong friends of mine stopped by to pray with us. In the hall afterward I asked them to specifically pray for the baby's passage from this life and his entrance into heaven. I knew I needed to focus on Eva, and I desperately wanted someone to be "holding" this precious little being in prayer. They pledged to do so.

My phone—busy all day with e-mails and texts and prayers—began to buzz. Karen was texting. I read a few lines and then looked up to ask if I could read her words aloud. Eva and Jason nodded. "This is so messed up!" Karen wrote in raw honesty. "But watch for God to show up. He will."

Then I checked my e-mails. There was an e-mail from Merideth. "Elisa, this may seem really weird to you right now, but if Eva and Jason would like photographs of the baby, I would be honored to come and take them. I do this for Now I Lay Me Down to Sleep, a nonprofit for such situations. Just let me know." I read her offer out loud.

Jason shook his head. "We've already decided—no pictures."

Eva looked up at him standing next to her. "I don't know, Babe. I kinda want her to come and take them."

Jason hesitated. I realized a connection and spoke it: "You know that giant picture of our family in our house? Merideth took it. And the ones of Marcus in your bedroom? Merideth took those too. Now that I think of it, she's our family photographer."

Jason nodded. Eva laid her cheek on his hand. I asked Merideth to come. I went out to find Salina, the nurse, to make plans. She led me to an empty room across the hall, where a warming table was set up. There was a hospital bed—a patient's bed—in the room as well. And its sheets were rumpled as if someone had just left them. I asked about it and Salina told me, "Oh, that's where Dr. G is sleeping."

"She's here?"

"Yes, she wanted to be close by for Eva."

Impressive. Maybe she wasn't so bad . . .

It was midnight when the labor climaxed. Ethan left for the waiting room as Dr. G entered the room and began the difficult chore of bringing a baby forth. "This will be hard. There will likely be no noise and if there is, it will likely be only for a minute." We three looked at each other. Eva was in full pain by now. For long minutes she pushed and panted. At one point she cried out, "I'm doing this for *nothing!*" I stood in awe as my brave daughter strained against her husband's arms and her body yielded forth a silent, still son.

Dr. G wrapped him in that blue hospital paper stuff and handed him to the nurse, looking at me as she said, "Don't look now. This is too hard. Let Salina clean him up." My heart snapped *no!* and I looked at Eva. She felt it too.

"Can I go with the baby?" I asked her. I knew I shouldn't be in the room with these newly grieving parents. It was *their* sacred moment. And I also knew that baby shouldn't be alone. Eva quickly nodded. But Dr. G put out her hand to stop me. "This is too hard," she said firmly.

Strength to strength, I met her gaze. "I can do this," I replied and I followed Salina out of the room and across the hall to the waiting warming table, its light on in preparation even though there was nothing to warm.

Salina gently laid the baby down, met my eyes, and said, "Take your time. Merideth is in the hall. Let us know when you are ready."

I turned my eyes from hers to the treasure on display before me. Tiny! Oh, and I'd thought Thomas had been tiny! Perfect! Perfect fingers and nose and ears and toes. His right arm curled about his head, lifting praise toward heaven. *Beautiful.*

Yet as instantly as I took in his beauty, I also realized his fragility. Tissue-paper skin. Sunken lungs. Delicate limbs. There was no way he could have lived in this world. He was not made for it. He was made for another world. I wept at his very being. I loved over him with a joy that comes from strangely but fully *knowing* another being. I prayed him fully alive in the arms of his Creator.

As I turned away I felt an immediate presence behind me—a hovering around my head. As if my eyes saw backward, I saw him rise from the warming table and *fly* to me, following me. He had *wings.*

Of course, when I turned around, he remained lifeless and unmoving. But as soon as I turned about again, he was there, hummingbird-like, about me.

As Merideth began her sacred work, I hovered in the hallway myself. I'd completely overlooked the reality that Eva would also need to deliver the placenta. What a torturous joke! An echo of suffering yet with nothing to show for it. I noticed a ribbon taped to the hallway room number. Purple. Not pink. Not blue. Purple. A warning to all hospital personnel who entered: Pain Within. Then, through the half-drawn curtain in her doorway, I took in my daughter straining, Jason cooing comfort, and the doctor instructing.

Dr. G's face was a question mark as she looked up at Eva and asked, "What will you name him?"

Jason said, "Oh, we decided we wouldn't name him."

The doctor responded, "I have to push back on that, Jason. He's a real life. He needs a name."

Jason turned to Eva. From my peeping spot I saw her look up at her husband as she asked, "How about Malachi?"

Air wheezed out of me as I watched Jason nod. Really? Malachi. The winged-one hovered behind me, smiling.

When Eva had recovered enough, Salina presented a swaddled Malachi to her and for just a few seconds, they were mother and child. Then with tears streaming, Eva held him out to me to take.

He weighed—nothing. He was air. Yet his being had such *reality*. What a privilege to steward his presence on this planet.

Back in the room across the hall, Dr. G was suddenly sitting by us, Malachi and me. I asked, "Really—what happened? Why would he just come at twenty-two weeks? What went wrong?"

"We don't always know. It could have been an infection in the womb, but we don't know."

"How often does this happen?"

"Practically never. But at this age, babies just don't survive," she answered.

The next morning, with three hours of sleep, I drove back to the hospital. On my way I called Karen—to fill her in on all that had happened. To tell her about the horrendous mess—but also about the way God had indeed "shown up." Merideth and the pictures. Malachi's name. His wings.

Jason had left to run some errands for Eva, so when I entered her room she was alone. A stunned shock had settled her face into exhaustion. We sat quietly talking. My pastor called and prayed. And then my phone began to buzz again. It was a lengthy text from Karen. I read the first few lines and stopped, my eyesight too blurred to continue.

I looked up at Eva. "Listen to this!" At that point Eva didn't even know Karen, but she listened anyway.

Sit down. Sit down now. You are not going to believe what I'm about to tell you. I hung up from talking to you just now and was walking into my church, into Bible study. My friend

Rachel saw me and came up and asked me what was going on. She said I looked stricken.

I told her I'd been in a "Bryant" moment since the day before. [Bryant was Karen's baby who lived only one hour and then died, some ten years prior.] That a friend—well the mother was the friend—but her daughter had just lost her baby the night before.

I knew Rachel would understand such stuff because she was my doctor when Bryant died. She actually started coming to Bible study with me because of that experience.

Then Rachel asked me my friend's name—the daughter's name—and she asked me what hospital.

I told her.

Rachel sucked air and said, "I'm the doctor. I delivered Malachi last night. I delivered Bryant, and I delivered Malachi."

Eva's mouth fell open.

A few minutes later the phone in the hospital room rang. It was Dr. G. *Rachel.* I answered. She blurted out, "I'm so sorry I didn't know who you were last night! Can I talk with Eva please?"

And she unleashed to Eva, "I need to come and see you right now! I really messed up last night and I need to ask your forgiveness. I should have asked you about your faith. I should have prayed with you and Jason. I'm coming right now."

Jason and Ethan returned with lunch as Dr. G entered the room again. She took all our hands and prayed. She'd brought Eva a verse . . . .

After hugs and more tears and more hugs, Dr. G approached me, took my hands, looked me straight in the eyes and said, "She did what she could." (She was referencing a book I'd written.) "I've heard you speak. Thanks for doing what you could last night."

By the time I got home that afternoon I was mush. Just a scoop of slop. I lay on my bed and picked up a book someone had dropped off for me. *Heaven Is for Real.* It's the story of Colton Burpo who "dies" at age three during an appendectomy, goes to heaven for a bit, and then lives. "Everybody's got wings," he writes.[1]

I close the book, shut my eyes, and he—Malachi—hovers, present with me. He still is.

Later I came across a quote from Eugene Peterson in *Living the Message*:

> It is essential to distinguish between hoping and wishing. They are not the same thing.
>
> Wishing is something all of us do. It projects what we want or think we need into the future.... Hope desires what God is going to do—and we don't yet know what that is.
>
> Wishing grows out of our egos; hope grows out of our faith.... Wishing has to do with what I want in things or people or God; hope has to do with what God wants in me and the world of things and people beyond me.[2]

I wish I had more faith to understand this, but I hold on to it nonetheless.

Eva hates it when I "preach" meaning into Malachi's life and death. "Mom. You always have to put a bow on everything!" I understand. She is his mother, after all, and her heart will forever ache with his absence.

But for a short sliver of time, I, too, became Malachi's steward. Of his being and his presence and his memory. The name Malachi means *messenger.* God sent us a messenger to speak to us a message he wants us never to forget. Life is messed up at times. But we are to watch for God even there. He does show up.

I turn to the comfort of the hereafter provided in Isaiah 65:17–20: "Look, I will make new heavens and a new earth, and people will not remember the past or think about those things. My people will be happy forever because of the things I will make. I will make a Jerusalem that is full of joy, and I will make her people a delight.... There will never be a baby from that city who lives only a few days."

In my personal universe, it is impossible for me to parent without faith. Faith holds me. Faith sustains me. Faith defines me. Faith carries me on wings.

....

Hope is a golden cord connecting you to heaven.

—SARAH YOUNG[3]

Five

I have five grandchildren.

No, I have one.

No—five.

But I can know only one because only one is here with me—on this planet—in my life.

He is the most amazing being, as if he is making up for the four he doesn't know but must somehow represent.

Five Christmas stockings are one.

Five school programs, sports events, trick-or-treats, Easter egg hunts, first days of school.

Five birthdays. No . . . two birthdays. One relinquishment ceremony. Three entrance-to-heaven days.

Like five fingers on a hand where only one is functional.

My Thanksgiving table is filled to full with the one. But there are moments when it yawns with four empty chairs. My arms wrap about the one and embrace all that life could offer. It is unimaginable that there could ever be more. Yet I reach for what I cannot hold.

12

Love

Mother pulled the bobby pins from our pin curls and brushed our hair smooth. Cathy's glistened blonde. Mine fluffed brunette. Next my sister and I stepped into matching petticoats, white tutus supported by strong elastic. Then came the ruffled anklets and the black patent leather shoes. Hers were three sizes larger than mine—and her shoes sported a convertible strap that could slide back over the heel and disappear, very grown-up like. My strap stayed in place over my preschool feet, holding them sturdily in my shoes. Finally the dresses: sheer pastel confections. Hers with puffed sleeves and a gathered waist. Mine more tailored with a wide-bodice collar.

It was March 1960, and my sister, Cathy, and I were being readied for the country club Easter egg hunt in our Atlanta suburb. The grand prize was a golden egg, presented to the lucky boy and girl who, after scrambling hither and yon over the golf course, found it and brought it safely back to the judge.

We arrived as a family, Daddy, Mother, Cathy, and me. The

beginning of brother Kirby was barely visible beneath Mother's tulip-printed maternity smock. Front and center at the starting line stood the country club president, presiding in his red seer-sucker blazer and holding two enormous stuffed Easter bunnies. One yellow for the girl winner. One orange for the boy. We posed for a few pictures with the family Brownie camera before lining up with our brightly colored wicker baskets and freezing for the whistle to blow to set us loose. Then, ignoring our Sunday school dresses, we galloped off, legs flying, hair whirling, tongues panting in search of treasure.

I remember eggs racing beneath me as I sped after the prize. Yellow. Orange. Pink. Purple. Plastic cases that held what I knew was a single nuggety sugar rabbit—the 1960s version of today's Peeps. I didn't much care for those nuggety sugar rabbits. Besides, I wanted to *win*. Winning meant finding one egg: the golden one. Winning meant the yellow stuffed Easter bunny would be mine.

As I ran, basket in hand, I let my eyes roam above the grass to the other searching children. I was a long ways out by now, and there were fewer children around me. Fewer eggs as well. Slowing to a trot, I squinted and scanned the ground ahead and to the sides of me. I stopped and looked back from where I'd come. Only a few eggs dotted the lawn of the golf course, and they were being snatched up quickly by the remaining foraging children.

My basket was empty still. Figuring that maybe I'd missed a section of the hunt, I retraced my path down the hill and ran up another mound. As I scaled the top, a group of people appeared before me. My father. My mother. A little boy and his parents. The judge holding the two enormous stuffed Easter bunnies. And my sister.

In her hand was a golden egg and on her face was a smile as broad as the arch of her basket handle. Cathy had found the golden egg.

The crowd gathered around and the judge cleared his throat.

Triumphantly, he presented the orange bunny to the successful boy and the yellow bunny to the winning girl: my beaming sister. Daddy and Mother looked on, happily clapping.

My eyes narrowed as I took in the scene. My throat tightened. I went cold. It was bad enough that I hadn't found the golden egg, but I'd never imagined that I might lose to my sister. I felt betrayed. Angry. Jealous.

The post-hunt pictures show a pouty me, arms dangling despondently at my sides, one hand holding a still empty basket, and my smiling sister, father, and mother. The brattiness seeps from the now-sepia pose. And the devastation. It is the last picture I have that was taken before the divorce.

Cathy is two years older than me. My older sister. She was there when I began and is there still. But for years and years and years, she didn't *feel* like my older sister. I wasn't sure she loved me, and honestly, I wasn't sure whether I loved her or what sister-love even meant.

....

From the get-go, Cathy and I were dressed in matching yet different outfits. At Christmas when the cowboy boots were unwrapped, hers were green and mine blue. For family portraits she wore pink and me blue. Grandmother Munna knitted us matching sweaters—differing colors of yellow and purply-pink. Cathy liked dogs. I liked cats. Cathy liked science and she also liked to read. I liked English and words and had very little interest in science. Cathy played volleyball. I was a cheerleader. We were different but the same. Sisters.

When our parents divorced, Cathy and I equally experienced the shredding of our worlds, yet our little girl hearts interpreted events differently, and we responded uniquely. As I've described, I became all-invested in "saving" my family. I stuffed my feelings down deep inside and focused on perfecting the role of fixer. Two years older than I, Cathy led with anger. She felt utterly abandoned by our father, stuck with our mother, and she coped with a resentful belligerence. These descriptions of myself and my sister match the prototypes of "Hero" and "Lost Child" in the Adult Child of an Alcoholic (ACOA) family role responses. I rose to lead. Cathy left in a huff.

To be honest, I don't remember her as being angry. She just was . . . you know, my sister. Other family members, older and beyond us, have shown me this perspective. What I do remember is our catfights, where—claws bared—we went after each other and had to be pried apart and have the fingernails withdrawn from each other's forearms. I remember the moon-sliver scars that remained for days—a kind of necessary hurt.

On our five-hour-long car trips from Houston to Fort Worth to see our grandparents, Munna and Bop, our baby brother, Kirby, was relegated to the front seat with Mother, and Cathy and I took over the back. With the two cats (we now both had cats in addition to our family dog)—and their litter pan. Really—who would *ever* think a cat would actually use a litter box in the back of a Chevy Impala? Mother. Instead, those cats panted from their perch on the back shelf of the car as we sped north down the highway. Before Cathy and I settled into our spots on the bench seat, though, we drew a clear line across the middle, prohibiting one from infringing on the other's territory. And then she escaped into her book—always a book. *Nancy Drew, The Hobbit, The Lord of the Rings*, Ray Bradbury—pretty heady stuff. I looked out the window and wrote myself into a million scenarios of drama and excitement as the miles passed beneath us. When her feet came near me, I'd emerge from my imaginings and swat them away.

We were nice to each other. Always pretty much pleasant. Sharing a bathroom requires a certain politeness. But she didn't value my fastidious tidiness, so in my cleaning routine, I often just shoved her bottles and potions into a corner, not caring whether they landed upright or not in the process. And she pretty much ignored my silent and verbal pleas for help with Mother and our brother, Kirby, who was just a kid and desperately needed guidance. It's like the whole family drama scene didn't register to her.

In her teen years, her leaving from the family became more pronounced. She went further away and for longer periods at a time. With school. With activities. With boys. More and more time away from home, returning later and later at nights. She left me alone with everything, it seemed. She's always been taller than me, but I can remember gazing—quite adoringly—at her prom-prepared updo as she pinned a boutonniere to her date's lapel and Mother snapped a photo. I wanted to know how she did her hair like that. But I held back from actually asking. I guess I didn't think she'd tell me. Or maybe I didn't want her to know I wanted something from her, as if it would give her power over me.

Like winning a golden egg.

One place we shared was church—and the youth choir, a hip, Jesus-loving group that typified the 1970s. We both fell in love with God through Young Life and our church. But as she was more into music than I was and I was more into Bible study than she was, we went our similar but different ways. She thrived in the choir. I was ordained as an elder.

Then eventually she left home for good. She left for college—to Vanderbilt University in Tennessee—whole states removed from us. Her Sunday afternoon newsy phone calls intrigued me. There seemed to be so much happening in her life! She pledged a sorority. She found a boyfriend. She lived in a dorm room and then in an apartment with a girlfriend.

All the while I was at home with Mother and Kirby, moored

to their needs and braced to hold what seemed to be the entire universe on my shoulders. While I understood that it was *time* for her to launch and sail away, something in me felt further abandoned. My big sister just didn't feel big, wiser, mentor-ish to me. She felt absent. Gone. Didn't love mean *staying?* Like my father hadn't. Like my mother couldn't.

Through our remaining growing-up years, we did some sisterly things together. I overnighted with her on my own drives across the country to college and we were, for the evening, college girls together. We both returned home for Christmases with Mother and Kirby, who was still stuck there in high school. But even then, she was out with friends and I spent time with my boyfriend, so the sum total of our time together was pretty much Christmas Day.

She met her husband-to-be and invited me to be her maid of honor. I happily agreed to the role and to the outfit she crafted—a very grown-up, long, navy-ish jersey dress. Her seamstress skills blossomed after our grandmother Munna and she designed and sewed her own wedding dress, followed by banners for her church and quilts for her friends. When I married she was my matron of honor. A picture of us bending forehead to forehead shows her launching me—or us launching each other—into marriage.

The years passed. We each did similar but different family things like having babies—hers by birth, mine through adoption. We worked and wived and mothered in similar fashion while living in separate states. We cared about our brother, Kirby, deeply, but with varying degrees of involvement. And we each returned to visit Mother—however, usually at different occasions and for different purposes.

In the summer of 1990 Mother was diagnosed with cancer. The origin of the site was in her mouth, and she required surgery and radiation treatment. We three took turns visiting her in Fort Worth, where she'd moved to be closer to her own mother after we'd all gone off on our own. The months were difficult for us all. I remember the struggle I felt, thick into the creation of my second family, with Mother wanting and needing my care. Hadn't I taken care of her all my life? Even though I was already in therapy reevaluating the wrong conclusions I'd come to as a child, I was nowhere near finished with the process, nor was I able to understand all that she was asking of me. In fact, I was so heavily into a necessary separation from my mother that the mere thought of a return to her snapped my fragile peace like a broken rubber band. When she asked for care—needed care—my heart recoiled. I didn't know how to care for her while choosing health for myself. From their own corners of the world, Cathy and Kirby were also working through their own issues with Paige, our mother.

At Christmas that year, Mother called to wish me Merry Christmas (she'd not been well enough to join us in Denver) and blurted out the news that the cancer had spread. To her backbone and rib. Not exactly holiday cheer. I was devastated. As much as I'd leaned away from her in order to *live* myself, I loved my mother deeply. I didn't want her to die. I hated that she was in pain.

A few weeks later Cathy, Kirby, and I met in our mother's small townhome in Fort Worth to go over the plan for her final days. One amazing thing about Paige: she was not afraid of death, and she was not one to avoid making the necessary arrangements. In between doctor visits and treatments, we sat on her couch—the same white couch she'd sat on way back in California after her divorce, with smoke circling up from the ashtray on the adjacent end table—and made to-do lists. We discussed end-of-life care: She didn't want heroic efforts to be employed. She agreed to a stomach tube for feeding if necessary for a while. She had a living will. She agreed to hospice care. (She wouldn't live long enough to need most of these arrangements.) Then we discussed the mortuary and memorial service. She shared her preferred minister, scriptures, flowers, and reception at Munna's. She wanted us to find a specific poetry book, *Altars Under the Sky*, and a specific poem. We wrote it down. (Several weeks later when I was in that back bedroom at my mother's house, I laid my hand on the spine of that book, tucked backward into a small bookshelf, and Cathy called from the hospital to tell me Mother was gone.) And we discussed division of property: furniture, paperwork, silver, jewelry, dishware, and Christmas decorations. An estate sale for whatever wasn't wanted by any of us and then sale of the townhome. A three-way split of her humble financial assets.

Exhausted by her disease, Paige then went to bed for the duration of our visit while we went to work going through cabinets and drawers and closets and stickering everything into colors: green for Cathy, blue for Elisa, red for Kirby, white for giveaway.

One afternoon we came to the closet with the Christmas decorations. Actually, Cathy came to it and hollered for Kirby and me to join her in the bedroom, where we sat on the two twin beds as she opened box after box of ornaments. A blue paper honeycomb bird spackled with glitter. Kindergarten egg-carton dangles. Broomstick angels. Clip-on ornament birds with white horsehair tails. Green for Cathy. Blue for Elisa. Red for Kirby.

We sorted them into piles and then into boxes. When a favorite one-of-a-kind bauble was unwrapped, we sat and held it, rehearsing its origin and lifetime, and then looked from one face to another to try to discern who wanted it the most. Usually the other two gladly relinquished the item to the one, but when there was a tug-of-war we put those items into a new pile to which we later returned and divvied them up in a fair and even manner. Such civility and respect.

Our hearts were heavy and there was much—so very much—left to be done before we returned to husbands, children, and work.

Later that night Cathy was back in the twin-bedded room, talking to her family on the phone. As she hung up I went in to get ready for bed and paused to sit next to her. It was a moment where our whole lives—all thirty-something years each—seemed to hang around us in the room.

"Why did you leave me alone with her?" I asked. The question had formed in the front of my mind in the days we'd been disassembling Mother's life, but it had been being shaped in the months of work I'd been doing with my counselor back in Denver.

Cathy didn't hesitate. She looked straight at me and said with clarity, "I had to leave, Elisa. If I hadn't left, I would have lost *me*. I didn't have a choice if I wanted to live. I had to leave for *me*. I had to find *me*."

The golden egg.

Finally. My sister's words made perfect sense. In that moment and ever since.

We two had survived a traumatic upbringing. The same broken family. But we'd chosen different escape routes—which really had nothing to do with loving or not loving. My survival meant staying and saving—trying to fix what was broken. Cathy's survival meant fleeing from what she had lost to find herself.

Green. Blue. Brunette. Blonde. We are the same, but different.

Paige has been gone for over twenty years now. She was young when she left, and we were very young when we let her go. We've had another lifetime to live as sisters, and prayerfully there will be more years to come.

Know what I've learned? We are still different. For sure. But also the same. Cathy holds double master's degrees and teaches prekindergarteners in a special-needs classroom. I spent the bulk of my career working with the moms of such an audience. I also hold a master's degree—just one. She is no longer married and has launched two amazing children. I am married still and continue to release my children as they find their ways. She's kind of a "reverse snob" and prefers the simplest of surroundings. I enjoy fancy stuff. We both love Jesus.

The "body of Christ" metaphor from 1 Corinthians 12:12 echoes forth. "The body is a unit, though it is made up of many parts; and though all its parts are many, they form one body" (NIV). We are the same, but different.

I've also learned this: relationships can change. In fact, relationships often have to change because we change. As sisters. And brothers. As wives and husbands. As daughters and sons and mothers and fathers. Relationships change if we let them, and if we do the work to reinvest in what they can become.

And I've learned that love can only survive and thrive if *we* find a way to survive and thrive. That growth toward health takes time. And that sometimes we have to *leave* in order to be able to *stay*.

I take to heart the words from the hotel owner, Sonny, in the film *The Best Exotic Marigold Hotel*: "Everything will be all right in the end. So if it is not all right, it is not yet the end."[1] In Elisaese that sentiment goes this way: We're not done until we're dead. If we're not dead, we're not done.

Such realities of sameness and difference, of growing and changing and leaving, of gaining and losing in life—these *family* realities shape us and make us who we are. Over a lifetime.

Judith Viorst writes of this process in her classic book *Necessary Losses*:

> When we think of loss we think of the loss through death, of people we love. But loss is a far more encompassing theme in our life. For we lose not only through death, but also by

leaving and being left. By changing and letting go and moving on. And our losses include not only our separations and departures from those we love, but our conscious and unconscious losses of romantic dreams, impossible expectations, illusions of freedom and power, illusions of safety—and the loss of our own younger self, the self that thought it always would be unwrinkled and invulnerable and immortal.

Somewhat wrinkled, highly vulnerable and non-negotiably mortal, I have been examining these losses. These lifelong losses. These necessary losses. These losses we confront when we are confronted by the inescapable fact . . .

that our mother is going to leave us, and we will leave her;

that our mother's love can never be ours alone;

that what hurts us cannot always be kissed and made better;

that we are essentially out here on our own;

that we will have to accept—in other people and ourselves— the mingling of love with hate, of the good with the bad;

that no matter how wise and beautiful and charming a girl may be, she still cannot grow up to marry her dad;

that our options are constricted by anatomy and guilt;

that there are flaws in every human connection;

that our status on this planet is implacably impermanent;

and that we are utterly powerless to offer ourselves or those we love protection—protection from danger and pain, from the inroads of time, from the coming of age, from the coming of death; protection from our necessary losses.

These losses are a part of life—universal, unavoidable, inexorable. And these losses are necessary because we grow by losing and leaving and letting go.[2]

Not long ago Cathy's eldest married. I met up with my sister, and we spent twenty-four hours selecting the perfect mother-of-the-groom dress, a silvery swirl of celery. The weekend of the wedding Kirby and Evan and I flew across the country to spread vivid yellow tablecloths on rented round tables and stick candles in pots of petunias for the rehearsal dinner, where Cathy presided as hostess with the mostest. Our calendars hold an upcoming date when we three siblings will go to Disney World to celebrate a milestone birthday together.

There's more ahead. More layers of life and therefore of love. Green. Blue. Golden.

....

Drink deep and full of the love of God and you will not demand the impossible from earth's loves; then the love of wife and child, of husband and friend, will grow holier and healthier and simpler and grander.

—OSWALD CHAMBERS[3]

Hands

My mother had died, and now her brother had also predeceased their mother—our grandmother. There was very little to keep the three of us siblings connected as the generations were inevitably passing. Only our grandmother, Munna, remained. And soon, she too would be gone. As we stood in her nursing home room, two sisters and a brother took our Munna's hands and wept as we shared of her only son's memorial service that she'd been unable to attend.

She had no words.

Two years prior, through a stroke, Munna had lost her voice and all movement except some use of one arm.

A silence settled over the room. We looked at each other, then at Munna, angled to sitting in her hospital bed. She moved that arm, first clutching my sister's hand and bringing it to rest on her lacy bed coat, over her heart. Next she reached for my brother's hand, guiding it atop my sister's. With eyes steeled, she reached for my hand and brought it to the other two, putting it in place. Once so arranged, Munna patted our three hands beneath her own.

We looked at each other.

When she moved her hand away, we moved ours away as well. One of us coughed, I think. It was awkward.

Instantly, she repeated her sermon, one hand at a time. My sister's. My brother's. Mine. One on top of the next until we formed a sibling pyramid. She patted. And patted. And patted once more just to make sure we were listening. Taking notes.

Without words, my grandmother preached a silent sermon. We listened. We remember. We hold her message in our hands today.

13

Respect

My best friend—other than my husband—is gay—and loves Jesus.

He told me when he was thirteen and I was eighteen. My response? I turned to Romans 1:18–28 and read aloud to him: "The wrath of God is being revealed from heaven against all the godlessness and wickedness of men who suppress the truth by their wickedness... For although they knew God... their foolish hearts were darkened ... Therefore God gave them over in the sinful desires of their hearts to sexual impurity for the degrading of their bodies with one another..." (NIV).

I'd never suspected. Well, maybe not never, but not really. Such things were not discussed in our middle-class suburban world. Heavens, we didn't talk about our mom's drinking, about not having enough money to pay our bills some months, about the cat hairballs in the breakfast room that remained encrusted on the knotty pine planks, about Ajaxing ashtrays to remove the soot, about seeing our father only once a year, about the cigarette burn spot underneath the carefully splayed magazines on the coffee table. Why would we chat it up about homosexuality?

He cried as he told me.

I read louder. "They exchanged the truth of God for a lie . . . Because of this, God gave them over to shameful lusts . . ." (NIV).

Looking back I recognize the s-word (*shame*) at work in that conversation. As he described how long he'd felt what he'd felt, how much he'd tried not to feel it, how many times he'd pushed to feel differently, shame bubbled up inside me. It must have been my doing.

Kirby is my brother, five and a half years younger. Because of our father's absence and our mother's alcoholism, none of us really had much parenting. But Kirby got the stub of the stick. He was only six months old when they divorced. While my older sister and I were old enough to attend the annual stilted steak dinners when my father traveled to see us, Kirby was too young and stayed home with Paige.

As my sister coped with her anguished abandonment by leaving home and not looking back—the stereotypical Adult Child of an Alcoholic "Lost Child" role—my heart turned toward the "Hero." It's certainly not that I was more mature or competent to carry such a load on my feeble shoulders. Rather, I was desperate enough to think I could fix things and make my family whole. I set my sights on cleaning our house every week, on fluffing up my bedroom into a safe haven, and on mothering Kirby.

Saturday mornings I made him the breakfast of his choice: pancakes, fried eggs, or a dish I thought I invented but have since discovered belongs to the South as a specialty: fried bologna. We played Monopoly and rode bikes and sat in front of Houston's local kids' television show, *Cadet Don*, with bowls of mounded scoops of ice cream and chocolate chip cookies. While I invented nicknames like Kirby Werby Dirty Face to describe his ever-present food-smudged mouth, no one else was permitted to defame him.

I was the closest thing to a parent Kirby had in those days. So, I reasoned, if he was gay, it had to be my fault. Sociologist Brene Brown writes, "Parenting is a shame minefield. Not only do we hang our self-worth on how we are perceived as parents but we hang a big part of it on how our children are perceived."[1] It didn't matter that I was only eighteen years old. As I saw myself at that time as Kirby's "parent," I was failing big time.

Shame—a crazy, not-true testimony of inadequacy and responsibility—has haunted me most of my life. It messes with my mind still. It locks me up in a box of my own condemnation, barring me from receiving the freedom God offers me.

When my brother and I waded into that first conversation about his sexual orientation, I had already left home for college and was back on a school break. I sat on my blue-and-white great-grandmother-created twin quilt at the head of the bed, Kirby at the foot, a sea of family heritage between us. I remember my mind grasping for answers, reaching for formulas to keep myself afloat. We both knew Jesus by then, so it made sense that my fingers would clutch the pages of Scripture like a life raft. Surely he hadn't read the passages. If he heard them, he would change his mind. It seemed so clear to me then.

And for the next decade or so, this was my approach: fix him. Like I tried to fix all things broken in my family.

Those years were tense. As an adult, Kirby moved to Denver for a time and lived with Evan and me. I continued to mother him until he spoke up and told me to stop. That it was time to shift our relationship. He was a man, and I wasn't his mother. While I knew he was right, it was painful for me to change. I felt somehow diminished. And still like his life was my fault but that now I had to stop trying to fix him.

The word *respect* filtered through my thoughts. Technically respect is defined as esteem. Surely I esteemed and valued my brother. But there was something else at work in me. Maybe what was hitting me was the concept of dignity? Of realizing and integrating the reality that God himself honors us with the option of free will, to decide who we will be and what we will attach our lives to. Could I respect my brother?

He moved to Houston and then to San Francisco for work. I visited him now and then, meeting others like him. His friends. His coworkers. His community. On one visit we went to his church. We sang hymns and listened to the Word proclaimed and passed the offering plate, just as I would have done in my own body of believers. I sat in a pew taking in both singles and couples around me, clearly many who were same-sex. I prayed, *Oh, God! What do you think about this place?*

It was as if God placed a gentle hand on my shoulder as I received, *Elisa, what do you think I see as I look at the people in your church? They are filled with sin as well. Sin that I died to forgive.*

I looked around for the Exit sign. Not because I *wanted* to leave but because I thought I might be hit with a lightning bolt as I remembered Annie Dillard's words from *Teaching a Stone to Talk*:

Why do people in church seem like cheerful, brainless tourists on a packaged tour of the Absolute? Does anyone have the foggiest idea what sort of power we so blithely invoke? Or, as I suspect, does no one believe a word of it? The churches are children playing on the floor with their chemistry sets, mixing up a batch of TNT to kill a Sunday morning. It is madness to wear ladies' straw hats and velvet hats to church; we should all be wearing crash helmets. Ushers should issue life preservers and signal flares; they should lash us to our pews. For the sleeping god may wake someday and take offense,

or the waking god may draw us out to where we can never
return.[2]

By that time I was a seminary graduate. I was supposed
to have the answers to such gnarly struggles. I studied my
Bible again. The Old Testament was peppered with messed-up
people—kings and prophets and women and men—sinning
with and against each other. In the New Testament Jesus never
spoke of homosexuality—perhaps because his audience in the
New Testament was largely Jewish, a population less inclined
to struggle, or address a struggle, with homosexuality.[3] Jesus
talked about sin and sinners and planks and specks in our eyes
and of our need—*all of us*—for forgiveness. The apostle Paul,
called to the Gentiles, talked about same-sex relationships. But
what did he *really* mean when he wrote to the Roman and the
Corinthian churches back in their inaugural days? Were his
comments pointed at temple prostitution or rampant promiscu-
ity, or was he addressing all forms of same-sex relationships as
being against God's design?

I didn't get it. I still couldn't see how Romans 1 could allow
for same-sex relationships to be okay with God. I went to see a
respected, aged, studied professor. I asked what he thought. He
said, "I've studied and studied and studied the Word, begging
God to show me that same-sex relationships are okay with him.
I want to see it. But I just can't."

More years passed. Kirby and I continued to do much of life
together. He was a part of our family and we were his. He was
brilliantly witty and bright. His emotional intelligence entered
a room before he had his hand on the doorknob. He became more
and more successful, achieving a management level in the airline industry. As he flew about the world for work and for fun,
I went with him. Our relationship was once again easy, bonded,
fun, challenging. We were soul mates in so many ways.

Until one morning he called from his office in San Francisco, an edge in his voice. Our nation was abuzz with issues surrounding same-sex relationships, and Kirby lived in the hub of it all. "We need to talk. I need to know where you stand. I'm flying out to talk to you. Tomorrow." My mouth went dry. Never one to be comfortable with conflict, I winced.

Evan and I talked it through. While Evan also couldn't embrace a biblical acceptance of same-sex relationships, he'd always taken the position that God looks at Kirby the same way he looks at Evan. *All* of us fall short. *All* of us need the grace of God. He'd told Kirby this on several heart-sharing occasions, and they shared a close relationship.

No kidding. God doesn't ask any of us to clean up *before* we come to him. The cleanup happens as a result of knowing God. Obedience follows faith—not the other way around.

As if this needs to be driven home even more to me, I over-hear a woman chatting about her friend who's gay—and her response. She says, "It's not our call to respond to truth *for* another."

The next day I met Kirby at the airport and drove him to one of our favorite Denver restaurants, where over the next four hours we talked. Actually, he talked for about three hours. I listened. I took in point after point about his life, his faith, his journey. Bottom line: How could I believe what I believed and still love him?

I opened my mouth with my response. "Kirby, I understand your points, I think. And I also understand that you want me to respect your views."

"I do," he replied.

"But now I need to ask you to do the same. You say you love me, but you do not believe what I believe. I love you—even though I do not share your position. I need to ask you to respect my stance, my beliefs, and my views."

I continued, "As I process this with God, I feel he has said two things to me. First, have I told you what I believe on this subject? I have. And second, I believe God is asking me to embrace this reality: It is God's job to judge. It is my job to love you as he loves you. I love you."

In therapy I'd learned that intimacy doesn't mean believing the same thing or doing the same thing or feeling the same thing as another. Sameness doesn't make intimacy. Intimacy can grow on the ground of differences when respect is offered. Kirby and I didn't have to believe, feel, or do the same things in order to be intimately close.

It's been over thirty years since that conversation. Kirby and I are closer now than ever. We respect each other. We still talk and travel and connect and live life together. And we still view the subject of same-sex relationships differently.

I still try to figure out just what to do with him. Not who he is. I get that. More how he interprets who he is.

I'm not alone with this struggle. I know. One of my dearest friends has a son who is gay. I've known him since he was born and have watched and prayed as he's made his journey "out." So much of his angst has been about understanding his sexual orientation while trying to make sense of what that might mean for his faith. And vice versa. What's a mother to do?

Then there's another friend whose brother is gay. She worries over an upcoming holiday meal at her parents' home—where they'll all be gathered. Her parents want to include her brother and his partner. My friend cringes, squirming at the thought of her adolescent kids witnessing the mishmash around the table. "I don't want them to think I think this is *normal!*" she announces. But it is—normal. It happens all the time around all kinds of tables. What's a sister to do?

Once I preached on evangelism: on bringing the light of Jesus into our dark world, including homosexuality in a long list of "dark" things. Afterward a young mom approached me. "I have to let you know that it hurt me when you included homosexuality in your list of dark issues. I'm gay—and my partner and I attend here with our son." She gestured to the towheaded two-year-old in her arms. "If we can't come here to worship Jesus . . . where are we to go?"

Good question. Not long ago I read a blog post by the title, "Can I Come to Your Church? I'm Gay," written by a pastor who has struggled deeply with how to live out his faith on this subject. He writes, "The question isn't asked by an issue; it's asked by a person who matters deeply to Jesus. This question is the cry of every human heart: 'Will you love me and accept me, or will you reject me?'"[4] What's a pastor to do? Or church members?

A few years back Kirby traveled with Evan and me to Australia and New Zealand. Two weeks together was challenging but rich. As we drove from Christ Church to Queenstown, we looked across turquoise water at snowcapped mountain peaks. It was gorgeous. In my backseat perch, I reached for *Jesus Calling*, a devotional that I took everywhere, opened to the day's reading (January 18), and began to share aloud:

> I am leading you along the high road, but there are descents as well as ascents. In the distance you see snow-covered peaks glistening in brilliant sunlight. Your longing to reach those peaks is good, but you must not take shortcuts. Your assignment is to follow Me, allowing Me to direct your path. Let the heights beckon you onward, but stay close to Me.[5]

I looked up at the view of snow-covered peaks and marveled. We all did. Really? What timing! Evan suggested, "Do a search of how many references to snow-covered peaks there are in the book." My clever iPad revealed one: today's. We all marveled again.

Three people nestled in a compact car, driving on the "wrong side" of the road through the southern hemisphere, were so intricately and intimately connected to God and each other that he would honor us—respect us enough—to speak that specifically to us. Were we listening?

....

Just a few nights later Evan and I received a troubling call from home—thousands of miles away. Ethan had "slipped" again, and our home while we were gone was not a place he could be left alone. He had created a dangerous environment for himself—and for our home in our absence. Evan and I spent hours working through details to troubleshoot the situation from afar. Near the end of the negotiation, Kirby knocked on our hotel room to see if we were ready for dinner. We motioned him inside, where he heard for himself via speakerphone the dregs of the conversation.

At last we finished, and Evan sighed and suggested we put the matter behind us and head for dinner.

"Don't you want to pray or something?" Kirby asked.

I could read my weary husband's heart. No, he didn't really want to pray at that moment, and neither did I. Maybe later. But as Evan and I exchanged glances, we silently agreed that Kirby was right. We bowed our heads and prayed what was honestly an obligatory sentence or two.

There. Done. We lifted our heads. But Kirby wasn't. Done, that is.

"I want to pray too," he said. And pray he did. With tears streaming down his face, his voice breaking and his heart full, he cried out to our God for Ethan's safety and healing. On and on he went, compassion and sincerity and love pouring forth.

He closed, wiped his wet face, and we rose, connected again

by the raw mess of our lives.

As Kirby went to blow his nose, Evan took my hand and said, "I'm not sure I've ever heard a more tender and faithful prayer. And I have to admit, I couldn't have prayed that right now."

Me either. I squeezed "amen" into his hand.

....

There are places in our lives that only God can go.

—DONALD MILLER[6]

Fly Boy

The picture is in black-and-white but I see it in grays. Three of us: sister, brother, me. We are young, my sister and I—maybe ten and eight? He is a toddler between us.

While my older sister sits clear and independent, my arms wrap around my baby brother, creating a nest.

I focus on my hands. I hold him motherlike, as if he is my own child.

He is mine. Mine to carry. Mine to protect. Mine to teach and lead and train. Mine.

For years I hold him with my hands. Until—long into adulthood—he wriggles out from my grip, looks me squarely in the eye, and smiles in gratitude.

My heart splits. Grieved gladness. I open my hands and watch him fly.

Fly boy. Fly.

14

Forgiveness

A speck is one half of one person. Really, it is. Know how I found out?

When my father died, all six kids from his three marriages received an allotment of his fortune. Nothing out of the ordinary, really. Except that the six of us didn't receive an equal distribution of his estate. We were ranked, and money was distributed by order. What defined the ranking no one knew then, nor do we know now. Well, at least I don't.

I can guess. Birth order? Gender? Married or single? With or without progeny? Age? Not sure.

It was a painful season for all of us—both those ranked above and those ranked below. It's hard not to assign one's intrinsic value on the planet by such a definition!

After some consternation, I let it go, chalking it up to my dad's messed-up value system—the same dad who told me he wouldn't be able to love me until I was no longer financially dependent on him. I'd worked hard to attain that financially independent status. Even when we bought a house and dared to ask for a bridge loan from him, my husband was ever-careful that we pay him back with a healthy helping of interest.

My dad did eventually tell me, clearly, that he loved me. It just took awhile. In my twenties, I'd begun to work at updating our relationship as best I could from my end. I wrote and asked to meet with him at a business location where I knew he was headed. He agreed, and I was able to share his world of cocktail parties and dinners and even a brief tour of the property where we stayed. It was awkward as always, and at one point early in the weekend I excused myself, figuring he was done with me and ready to golf with his buddies instead. When I ran into my stepmom on my way back to my room she asked why I wasn't with my dad. I told her I thought he was "done" with me. She answered, "He may act like that Elisa, but he set aside the whole weekend to spend with you."

That got my attention. I realized he and I probably shared a great fear—though possibly from opposite angles. He was afraid to love. I was afraid to be loved. Looking back now I know that these fears are simply two sides of one coin. If you struggle with one, you probably struggle with the other.

In my room I read 1 John 4:18: "Where God's love is, there is no fear, because God's perfect love drives out fear. It is punishment that makes a person fear, so love is not made perfect in the person who fears." The verse echoed the reality that if Jesus had already endured all the punishment necessary to appease God for our mess-ups, I was denying his work by fearing. I prayed, yielded my fear, took a deep breath, and went in search of my father. That night over dinner I probed my father with questions, and he gave me honest answers. No magic cure for the lack of our relationship up to that point. But over the weekend new connections layered the once empty space between us. Questions.

Answers. Conversation. Presence. These things have a way of weaving ties that can eventually bind.

Over the years I kept at it: trying. I interviewed my older half brothers for their perspectives and carefully followed their advice. While I grew to expect the awkwardness of my relationship with my father, I began to believe that any involvement was better than none at all. On one visit in Florida, he floored me with a few sentences.

Evan and I had brought our two elementary-age kids to Orlando to do the normal Florida family stuff, and then we all scooted down to see my dad and stepmom in the southern part of the state. We had just finished dinner when Evan rose to take the dishes to my stepmom in the kitchen, and the kids followed, leaving just my dad and me. Alone. We sat in silence for a few minutes and then he plopped his napkin down on the empty table and said, "Money was always more important than you, Elisa. I'm sorry. I do love you. Will you forgive me?"

Will you forgive me?

The "pleaser" in me almost brushed off these four words like the crumbs from the table. I started to say something inane like, "No big deal." God stopped me. Really, it was him. He heart-whispered, *Elisa, you've been waiting all your life for this moment. Listen . . .*

And I did. I listened to my father's words. And I *heard.* His words fit like a perfect patch over a very old hole in my heart. I looked my Daddy in the eye and said, "I forgive you. Instead of wishing for what we didn't have, maybe we can enjoy what we do have now?" He nodded and patted my hand.

Over the next decade or so, my dad and I continued to form our relationship. It wasn't all I longed for—or all he wanted either, I'm sure. But it was. And that was good. Understandably, as my father aged and began to fail, I found my heart drawn even more intensely to him. I joined my stepmother for his first and second open-heart surgeries and prayed with them before both.

When he died, I was deeply grateful to be present holding his hand, praying in his ear, yearning that we would have more time together in heaven. But I don't really know where he ended up in his post-death world. At various times, I'd shared my faith in Jesus with him, early on in a pious and idealistic voice of youth and then later in the more down-to-earth words of a worn woman of faith. He'd believed in God but had spent most of his days holding on to his self-made stature. I discovered that he'd endured several forms of abuse in the poverty of his southern world. His own father had abandoned him when he was ten. He'd shouldered the load of providing for his mother and sisters by bagging groceries. I'm not sure he ever finished high school. That he'd risen to the top of a large corporation was incredibly impressive. He deserved to be proud. And eventually I grew to be proud of him as well.

As he died, I knew that he loved me. The distribution of his will testified of his love. Receiving any level of inheritance further defined me as loved by him. I was grateful for the work of forgiveness.

God has an interesting way of layering certain lessons in our lives.

....

Six years before my father's death, my mother passed into the next world. At her deathbed I watched her reach her hands out to Jesus, asking us if we could see him standing beside her. In that moment, all the pain she'd cast my way over the years began to abate. A true *knowing* settled into my soul. My mother hadn't meant to hurt me or disappoint me or abuse me. In so many areas of my life, she surely didn't give me what I needed from a mother. But looking back, I knew that she did what she could.

In the disassembly of her home and hearth, I reflected on the importance I assigned to the relics of her world that I brought home to Colorado with me. That sweet, small volume of poetry that my fingers had touched the moment my sister called from the hospital to tell me she had passed. The diamond from her wedding ring. An emerald green brocade, Barbie-like cocktail outfit that my grandmother had designed and crafted.

While Mother had evenly divided her modest estate between her three children, it was the artifacts of her life that held the most meaning to the three of us. The steadfast presence of certain *things* echoed the reality of our mother's love whispers. She *had* loved us so very much. It's just that her inability to cope with the life she was left with twisted her love into what wasn't love. And we couldn't hear it any more.

Weeks after her death and back home in Colorado, I was driving to the store when I glanced up through the windshield to the blue, cloud-speckled sky. A realization rippled through me: "You can *see* me now, can't you, Mother? You can *love* me now." I smiled. Now that was worth waiting for.

I began to forgive her. I continue forgiving her still.

Of all the broken family values, forgiveness may be the most essential to survival and beyond that, to creating a lasting family legacy. Both getting it—and giving it.

Getting forgiveness and giving forgiveness were not terribly hard in the first seasons of my faith. In my less-formed faith I leaned into a kind of simple obedience. If God told us to forgive, then I forgave. My boyfriend when he disappointed me. A teacher when she mispronounced my name over and over, again and again. My brother when he forgot to give me an important message. But in my adult years, I faltered in forgiveness. Maybe it's because adult sins—both committed and incurred—have bigger consequences? I'm not sure. Hard-to-forgive moments have left me splayed out in the dirt. Even when I've thought wounds past were forgiven and forgotten, they have infected and reinfected my relationships and choices.

I've had to return to the basics of forgiveness again in my adult years. My remedial course (taken just about every "semester" in my grown-up life) underlined what forgiveness isn't—and what it is.

Forgiveness doesn't mean overlooking a wrong. That's dishonest. It can also be damaging. Denial and rationalization don't heal hurts. They just bandage infection. You can't erase a wound by pretending you weren't injured. Neither is forgiveness excusing a wrong. That's removing blame. We don't have that power.

Forgiveness is looking square at an offense and seeing it for what it is. C. S. Lewis writes: "Real forgiveness means looking steadily at the sin, the sin that is left over without any excuse, after all allowances have been made, and seeing it in all its horror, dirt, meanness and malice, and nevertheless being wholly reconciled to the (person) who has done it."[1]

Hard stuff. For sure.

Applying forgiveness—truly *using* it in my daily relationships— has taught me there are two dimensions of forgiveness: getting it and giving it. These dimensions come in a one, two order. First one. Then the other. You can't give what you don't have. So in order to give forgiveness you have to first get it.

Regarding my parents, it didn't seem to me that I had much to ask forgiveness for. At least on the surface of things. The issue was more about me forgiving them, right? I was a child they didn't love well. It wasn't my fault that my father left or that my mother drank to excess. What did I have to be forgiven for? Being born? Living?

Yet the work I began in the dismantling season of my second family convinced me of my own need for forgiveness with my first family. Maybe I wasn't responsible for the breakage in my first family, but hadn't I contributed to the lack of healing in some ways? What had I done "wrong"? Well, how about hatred? Judgment? Anger? Resentment? Bitterness? Lifting the corner of the carpet, I discovered rotten planks in the knotty pine floor of my being. There was plenty that I needed to be forgiven for. And I couldn't forgive my parents if I didn't have access to forgiveness for myself.

So I bent my posture toward the "sinful woman's" in Luke 7, where Jesus is clear: "But the person who is forgiven only a little will love only a little" (v. 47). There's a connection between our understanding of our need to be forgiven and our ability to love others. Who loves God and others the most? Potentially, it's the biggest sinner! Who is best able to forgive others? The *forgiven* biggest sinner! Recognizing our sin doesn't disqualify us from loving and life—it actually equips us.

Real forgiveness—whether of someone who has wounded us or of our own sins—comes from God. God provides it. He cracks open his very heart and carves forgiveness into existence through the death of his Son on a cross. Then he welcomes us into the very center of his heart creation.

I couldn't give what I hadn't received. I had to get in order to give. I needed to be forgiven much in order to love much. Even with my mom and dad.

Another thing about forgiveness: Forgiveness has no limit and no expiration date, either for getting it or for giving it. Just as we can return again and again to get it, so we are to give it over and over and over. In Matthew 18, Peter asks Jesus, "How many times shall I forgive my brother when he sins against me? Up to seven times?" Jesus answered, "I tell you, you must forgive him more than seven times. You must forgive him even if he wrongs you seventy times seven" (Matthew 18:22). The point Jesus makes is that we are to forgive others not just seven times, but to infinity and beyond!

I get to see this reality played out in my relationships nearly every day. With my daughter. With my son. With my husband. With my sister. And my brother. With my extended half- and step-siblings. With myself. Oh—and with God too. Sometimes I'm in a spot where I actually have to forgive God even though he's surely done nothing wrong. But I *feel* like he has because he didn't prevent the thing that did happen from happening. Or he didn't bring about what I wanted him to bring about.

Forgiveness is unending and ongoing. Sometimes it seems as if it'll never penetrate the tough shield of my will. Months and years—even decades—pass and the gritty refusal digs in deep like a stubborn splinter under the skin. Until at last time works its way, the membrane softens and the plank loosens its hold. When I finally understand it's needed, I can go to the cross and get it in order to give it. Beautiful.

One more thing. Forgiveness means releasing my right to resentment.

People hurt us and we hurt others. Hurt people hurt people. This has been a reality since the fall of Adam and Eve. Classic literature tells stories of surprising forgiveness received and given in tales like *The Count of Monte Cristo* and Victor Hugo's *Les Misérables*. Memoirs from World War II tell of forgiveness given even in the face of the terrible trauma of the Holocaust: Elie Wiesel's *Night*, Corrie ten Boom's *The Hiding Place*, and in the Japanese POW camps, such as Laura Hillenbrand's tale of Louis Zamperini in *Unbroken*.

In this last book—a true story of forgiveness—prisoner of war Zamperini is stunned to discover, "The paradox of vengefulness is that it makes men dependent upon those who have harmed them, believing that their release from pain will come only when they make their tormentors suffer."[2] Author Hillenbrand nudges me forward. We hold on to pain because we want to control the punishment of those who've wounded us. But what happens is that they end up controlling us.

Bottom line, resentment happens when someone cuts off one of our arms and we decide to get even by cutting off our other one.

Instead of trying to get even or waiting for the wounding party to pay, R. T. Kendall believes "total forgiveness" is actually about being *for* another. "The ultimate proof of total forgiveness takes place when we sincerely petition the Father to let those who have hurt us off the hook—even if they have hurt not only us, but also those close to us."[3] And more: "Total forgiveness involves an additional element: praying for God's blessings to rain on the lives of your offenders."[4]

First my mother died. Then six years later, my father died, leaving me with one relative on the upper side: my stepmother. The parents I'd always wanted whole and healthy in my days were gone—and I was left with the one I'd never wanted. Because I felt she'd "stolen" my father from us, I held tightly to a bitter resentment of her continuing presence in our lives. Slowly I realized that she didn't deserve such treatment. While yes, she may have stepped too quickly into the shambles of a faltering marriage, she was loving and funny and fun.

Gradually God pried my prized resentment out of my hands and turned my heart toward forgiving her as well. I began to forge a friendship and upped my time investment in our relationship to travel to see her several times a year. When I arrived at her high-rise condo overlooking the gulf, she greeted me with a wide smile and a lilting *"Elisa!"* that made me all the more glad I'd made the effort. Over a glass of wine, I heard stories of her Appalachian upbringing, of her abusive first marriage, of her adoration of and protection for her daughter, and of the love of her life: my dad. By the time he died, they had been married nearly forty years. That had to count for something.

I learned to love my stepmother. I believe she loved me too. Forgiveness.

When she died, the bank sent out copies of her will, detailing every cent that went to every person in her world from her housekeeper to her nine hundred relatives I'd never heard of before (well, it *seemed* like nine hundred) and then, to her six kids—biological and step. No dollar amounts were mentioned. Instead, her estate was divided into "shares" with "parts" given to people. Thus, next to each person's name was a description of the percentage of the estate they would be awarded. Next to my name was the phrase: *one half of one part.*

I was a speck. I struggled all over again with just what such a distribution meant. Love me? Love me not?

It wasn't the allotment of money that stung. It was the ranking. Again. My stepmother had shaken her head at my father's distribution of wealth and the resulting apparent evaluation of his children. And then she'd repeated it herself. While some part of me guessed she was trying to rectify his wounding by her action, another part of me winced with her current assignment of my value. I was a speck.

Oh dear . . . I was still bitter.

I had more work to do. More fear to release. More love to receive. More forgiveness to get. More getting to give.

....

Every time God forgives us, God is saying that God's own rules do not matter as much as the relationship that God wants to create with us.

—Richard Rohr[5]

Some Reassembly Required

I knelt before the pressed wood pieces arranged on the rug before me. Some notched with bumps, some etched with holes, their fake-grain running in a horizontal direction. I must remember that: horizontal. It would be important for the end product.

Picking up the plastic bag of bolts and screws, I eyed the Allen wrench. Why was it called that? And why did I know it was called that? I tore open the bag with my teeth and matched each fastener to the illustration in the direction booklet—first turning it over to show English rather than Spanish. Yep, I had the correct number of As and Bs and Cs and—*geesh!*—the alphabet trailed across the paper all the way to RR. This would take a while.

My right foot was tingling. Too long in one position. But I had to get this done. The hutch was to hover over my file cabinets, housing the various business cards, pamphlets, books, and knickknacks I'd lugged home from my past life of leadership. In an office. With bookshelves. And a staff. I had to create some order from the acquired mess of twenty years.

Blowing out with determination, I rearranged my twisted body, picked up the electric screwdriver, and started in. An hour and a half later, the hutch stood upright on the ground in front of me, in one piece and apparently stable.

Voila! Proud Elisa stood back and took in my efforts.

Oops. The doors were upside down. Or were they inside out? I scoured the directions for the visual to show what the thing was supposed to look like. Rats. They were both upside down and inside out. And they were the one element of the fake furniture that required snazzy little spring hinges—that had been a *bear* to align and install. Ugh.

Some reassembly required. In the store, I'd read the words *Some assembly required* and hadn't thought much of it. Most stuff requires some steps to put together, right? But really? *Reassembly?* The thought seemed too much. I hadn't planned on extra effort in my afternoon. I was ready to stash my stuff in the hutch, wipe my hands, and move on to the next thing to be done.

But I wasn't done. So I wedged the point of the screwdriver back into the screw slot—such an expert by now—and reversed its drive to out instead of in. The hinge snapped in two and fell in my hand. Sitting back on my haunches, I peered at the now-useless hardware. Cheap. Undaunted, I tackled the second door. *Pop!* Number two hinge failed as well.

Now what?

I stood and stared at my doorless hutch. I'd planned on doors. Doors to hide the mess of random relics from my old life that I didn't have a place for in my new life. I wondered if I could find replacement hinges at the store. Right. The whole thing was shipped in a giant prefabricated carton from China.

Evan walked by. He *hates* putting stuff together and has repeatedly warned me not to count on him for help when I get such have-to-have ideas in my head. He paused, took in my doorless hutch, and said, "Looks pretty good!"

I decided he was right. It did. It didn't look like the picture on the carton, but it would work. It wouldn't hide my mess, but it would hold it.

15

Thankfulness

In our family, I've been partial to the Thanksgiving craft of handmade turkeys. You know, where you trace around your hand on a sheet of construction paper and cut out the pattern to form a turkey? We don't do this every single year—my family would object: "Oh, *Mom!*" But from time to time I trot out this tradition, sometimes just to get the conversation flowing around a table of family forced to eat with folks they don't know so well. And often I tack on an assignment: Name five things for which you are thankful—and share them around the table. One for each finger/feather.

In some years the thanks flow. Thank*full*ness. We burst with gratitude! A wedding is in the works. A fabulous job. Vacation just around the corner.

In others, someone—or everyone—is somberly silent. Not so sure what we're thankful for.

The family is broken. The home is foreclosed. The job is cut.

The significant other is suddenly not so significant. The country is going places we don't want to go.

Hard, I know. But honestly—can't we all come up with five things we're thankful for if we stop to really consider? We're breathing. We slept through the night. A golden-brown turkey awaits our gobbling. We have a roof over our heads. We should be *thankful.*

Thankfulness flows from stopping to see the obvious good things about us—and from searching for the not so obvious blessings in the making. Big. Small. Clear. Cloudy. Desired. Undesired.

One year—a particularly challenging holiday for our family—I thought it'd be a dandy idea to add an assignment to the turkey drawing. Instead of focusing on the "face up" fingers of what we're thankful for, I challenged us all to turn our turkeys over and to consider for a minute what we're *not* thankful for—yet what God still wants us to thank him for. When instead of being thankful we'd rather utter "No thanks . . ."

That year five such "no thanks" things came easily. I'm *not* thankful that my son is not at the table. I'm *not* thankful that my daughter was in a car accident and sits strapped into a clavicle device staring at her plate. I'm *not* thankful that it's blizzarding outside and the rest of our guests can't make it to our house so we sit numbly in our unusual smallness. I'm *not* thankful that things are so challenging at work and I'm not sure I have what's needed to sort them out. I'm *not* thankful that a month of holiday celebrations stretch in front of me—a season of merriness when I'm anything but.

The assignment proved much more difficult than I imagined. No thanks.

I remember John 13:30: "It was night." The phrase comes after Jesus hands bread to Judas, prophesying his betrayal, and after Judas leaves with his moneybag to do so. John writes that Satan had entered Judas. That Judas went out. And that it was night. The sentence stings. That's how I feel: a perpetual darkness descends. I'm not thankful.

I think about a phone call that came a few days earlier. A friend—okay, the chair of the board of MOPS International—called and rattled me with his question: "Have you thanked God in this yet?" *This* meaning my son's need for treatment. My daughter's accident. Our broken family. I stood with the phone to my ear, staring out my dining room window at the stick-dead trees. No signs of life.

What? What was he saying? Give thanks?

He repeated Paul's words from 1 Thessalonians 5:16–18 (NIV): "Be joyful always; pray continually; give thanks in all circumstances, for this is God's will for you in Christ Jesus."

Oh mercy. I mean, really. What was he saying?

If it had been someone else on the phone—really just about *any*one else—I would have wound my way out of the conversation with a wave of my to-do list and the upcoming table to prepare. (The table for, what would it be, *five?*) But this was Bob, my boss, and a man I knew who was well acquainted with grief. I sank down right where I was onto the carpet. I liked it there: on the carpet. The view was better from there. Soft cream pile in my face. I couldn't see the spidery branches.

There was silence on the phone while Bob waited. Finally I asked, "What do you mean?"

He answered, "We don't have to understand it. God just says to thank him. *In all* circumstances. That's what the verse says. Give thanks *in all* things. Because thanksgiving does something to us when we give it to God."

I didn't want to thank God. I wanted to gallop off and lasso my son and drag him home. I wanted to raise a magic wand, flip back the calendar pages, and erase the events surrounding my daughter's wreck. If I couldn't accomplish either change in my world, then I wanted to lay my head on the rug. *Forever.*

I felt Bob's gentle words digging under my armpits, raising me to my knees. So I tried. A mumbled "Thank you in this, even though I don't have a clue what you're doing, God," would have to do.

In the moment, it didn't seem to make a big difference. I pretty much dragged myself through the days that followed. But on Thanksgiving Day, seated at my scaled-down table with my miniature family feast, I turned my construction paper turkey over and contemplated what "no thanks" moments God might begin to inhabit if I named them—and then thanked him for allowing in my days:

No thanks #1: The absence of my son: Thank you that my son is at a faraway ranch in a program for his health. That while he is far away, he is safe. That there is a horse there that knows his voice and responds to his commands and that as he offers them, my son is learning that his actions influence others.

No thanks #2: The accident: Thank you that my daughter is alive. That she is seated at this table with us. That while she wears a sling, her heart is freshly held by you and she has more days on this planet to discover what your love looks like.

No thanks #3: The blizzard and therefore the tiny Thanksgiving table: Thank you that we are warm and snuggled in. That our extra friends are safe in their own home. That we sit together with one faithful couple that has chosen to courageously share our terror at the trials before us.

No thanks #4: The challenges at work: Thank you that I can't fix everything that is broken in the ministry where I serve. That challenges are often not about failing but about learning. That when we, as a staff, struggle, we grow closer together and closer to you. That you can use everything for your purposes.

No thanks #5: The long stretch of holiday celebrations ahead: Thank you for the advent of you, God. That you come and come and come, again and again and again, into my world and to my table by the window with the view of bare branches, assuring me that you will not leave me alone. Emmanuel. God with us. God with me.

I scrawled my construed thanksgiving across my fingers/ feathers and looked up to find the faces around me similarly pensive. We finished. Some of us spoke what we'd written. My daughter looked at her plate. We bowed our heads and my husband led us in "grace," acknowledging what we lacked before receiving what would meet our need.

Months later, my dear friend, coauthor, and coworker Carol called to tell me her husband was being airlifted from the mountains where they'd been vacationing to the in-town hospital. He'd collapsed with a horrific headache. The paramedics used words like "stroke" and "brain bleed."

As I sped across Denver to meet them in Boulder, I prayed and begged God to encourage my friend and to stabilize her husband. In the hours and days that followed, a surreal reality descended on their world. Would he ever be the same? Would he talk? Would he walk? Would he *be*?

We were standing outside the hospital entrance, seeking a bit of fresh air for Carol's muddled mind, when Bob—yes, the same Bob—walked up the drive on a visit to Carol. He hugged us both and then we sat together on a bench by the doorway. "Have you thanked God in this yet?" he asked Carol with all the sincerity of a pastor hosting communion. Carol's face registered the same disbelief I'm sure mine had shown back during my Thanksgiving preparations.

I listened as Bob explained. I watched as Carol struggled to comprehend. The three of us bowed and prayed, in varying degrees of faith, thanking God in the "this" before us.

Ann Voskamp remarks, "Count your blessings, not your hopes. Thanksgiving shapes a theology of trust."[1] In moments of waiting and wondering and straining and stretching, I've learned that the way we wait expresses the extent to which we trust the one we're waiting for. If I thank God in the midst of *all* circumstances, then I say to him and to myself and to anyone else who is listening that I trust him in the midst of *all* circumstances.

Years later, God leads me again to the power of thanksgiving. This time it's the middle of the summer when I read Sarah Young's *Jesus Calling*. I open to July 24: "Thankfulness opens the door to My Presence. Though I am always with you, I have gone to great measures to preserve your freedom of choice. I have placed a door between you and Me, and I have empowered you to open or close that door. There are many ways to open it, but a grateful attitude is one of the most effective."[2]

I make my "no thanks" list again. It is just as long. Maybe longer. I might need two hand-turkeys. I count: one, two, three, four, five, six, seven . . . No thanks. Thanks. Thanksgiving.

But—funny thing—when I look at my old "no thanks" list, I notice a surprising shift. Things that used to be on my "no thanks" list are now on my "thanks" list. They've moved from one list to the other. From *no thanks* I don't want my daughter to be pregnant to *thanks!* for my incredible grand*one*. From *no thanks* I don't want my son to struggle with addiction to *thanks!* he is so very honest and strident in his recovering life. From *no thanks!* I don't want the parents I had to *thanks!* my parents are exactly who I needed to shape me into the woman I am today, with the offering I bring to this world.

I give thanks—in all circumstances—believing that I will be changed in the process.

And I am. Thankful.

....

What's lost is nothing to what's found, and all the death that ever was, set next to life, would scarcely fill a cup.

—FREDERICK BUECHNER[3]

Net Gain

I backed up against the wall, placed my heels next to the baseboard, and flattened the curve of my back against the surface. Next came the pencil, held as straight as I could manage, eraser at the very crown of my head, lead point like an arrow aimed at the wall. I held my breath, careful to keep the pencil horizontal, scratched a mark, and moved away. How very satisfying it was to see the space between the present mark and the past mark. Even as a five-foot-two-inch fifth-grader, I *loved* to grow.

We are *born* to grow. There's something exhilarating about getting a driver's license, learning to navigate a new city after a move, sharing thoughts in a book club, mastering a program on the computer, completing an entire dinner with side dishes and getting it on the table—hot. Growing is good.

Yet, as a woman, growth is hard to track. In the mornings, I purpose to be kinder and gentler. By noon I'm still the "me" that isn't really either. I decide to invest in my friendships and then think up reasons that I can't possibly meet a friend after work or cut away in the middle of the day for lunch. I pick up a book and put it back on my nightstand after digesting only a single paragraph. I want to grow, but I find myself straining upward with no visible results for my effort.

Frustrated with my own apparent lack of growth, at times I've turned to measuring myself by the growth of my children. My life seems paralyzingly the same. Their progress? So much more rewarding! Shopping for the next year of school, my son jumps two sizes in jeans. Wow! Ordering me back from the doorway of her bedroom, my daughter announces, "I don't need you to put me to bed anymore, Mom. I'm too big for that." Amazing. How utterly satisfying it has been to transition a child from car seat to passenger seat to driver's seat.

But the thing is, once children move beyond the growth-chart stage, their growth becomes more difficult to measure. Their progress becomes less linear and more intrinsic.

My young-adult son moved out and went to college. I measured: plus five! The first semester his grades dipped: okay in two classes, not so good in two classes. I measured: negative four. The second semester he pulled up his grades . . . somewhat. Plus two! Then he moved home and began to take classes from a local school. Plus three. Then he decided to take a break . . .

I jumped to the conclusion that nothing was happening. Failure. Disappointment. Off track. In holding up my measuring tape to my son's apparent lack of growth, I've learned to re-examine my own. Perhaps the total pattern matters more than the isolated incident. The net gain is what you get when you add up all the ups and downs and still come out with something more than zero. It's not so much where you are but the direction you are heading.

Applying "net gain" to my own development, I look back— further than a week or two and deeper than the surface. I discover my heart is less worried about decisions made by others around me and more concerned with my own. When my husband returns from a business trip, I find that my mind turns not so quickly to my mental list of what I need him to do and more speedily to the image of his presence in the kitchen as I prepare dinner. I note that I ignore the shoes left on the stairs. Instead, my focus is on the heart of the young man who slid out of them in consideration for the dirty prints they might track on the carpet.

I back up against the wall to check my progress, and while I may move away, pencil in hand, with little noticeable difference in my mark today compared to my mark yesterday, I know I am still growing. I think this is God's growth goal for me: that I become more of what he intends for me to be—each day. A little bit more of some qualities today than yesterday. Somewhat less of others than the day before. Net gain.

Part Three

THE BEAUTY OF BROKEN

Three kinds of souls, three prayers:
1) I am a bow in your hands, Lord. Draw me, lest I rot.
2) Do not overdraw me, Lord. I shall break.
3) Overdraw me, Lord, and who cares if I break!

—NIKOS KAZANTZAKIS[1]

16

A Beautifully Broken Legacy

I knelt before the shambles of my Munna's antique plate collection and wept for the layered loss it represented in my life. There was no way I could fix any part of the mess. Each plate was broken beyond repair. The portrait plate of Marie Antoinette and its mate of Louis XVI. The scalloped-edged porcelain of painted yellow poppies. The latticed baroque. I swept the shards into a dustpan, walked them to the trash can, and trickled the contents inside, hearing them tinkle into even tinier pieces as they met each other's sharp edges.

When the hutch clattered off the wall in my dining room, spilling its treasured contents into ruin, I began my own toppling. For years I had poised my efforts to fix my first broken family and then to create a second family that would be immune from breakage. Despite my best efforts, my most sincere obedience to the ways of God and his Word, I still come from a broken family.

I lift my head, cock it just so, and finally begin to see the beauty in the broken.

Instead of my grandmother's antique plate collection, the artwork of broken family values now hangs on the walls in my home. *Commitment. Courage. Humility. Reality. Relinquishment. Diversity. Partnership. Faith. Love. Respect. Forgiveness. Thankfulness.* The litany of God's handiwork decorates my heart. *God hallows broken families. God holds broken families. God helps broken families. God heals broken families.*

There's no such thing as a perfect family. Every family is broken. Yours, mine, and ours.

So do we get in bed and pull the blankets up over our heads? Tempting. While we fantasize such an escape at times, in most of our homes, they're still out there—family members. They need to be fed and clothed and talked to and such. And even if they are grown and gone, we still have *life* waiting for us. We can't just go to bed.

But what *can* we do? What kind of family *can* we build? What kind of legacy *can* we leave?

One that is broken—and yet still beautiful. Or maybe a legacy that is beautiful *because* it's broken.

When we sit among the shards of our shattered hopes—fingering fragments that we know will simply not go back together again—we are just where God wants us. You see, he doesn't just sweep all our fragments into the dustpan and carry us to the trash. Into our breaking comes God's beauty. And through our breaking, God sculpts a beautifully broken legacy.

God has crafted an astounding element in beauty. Different cultures interpret beauty in various ways, evidenced by their multiple definitions of their word for beauty. In Hebrew, *yapha* means "glow, bloom." In Greek, *to kalon* is "idea or ideal." Sanskrit uses *sundara* to express "whole, holy." In Navajo, *hozho* is "health, harmony." English's *beauty* means "the object of longing."[1]

C. S. Lewis talks about this longing in *The Weight of Glory*: "We do not merely want to *see* beauty, though, God knows, even that is bounty enough. We want something else which can hardly be put into words—to be united with the beauty we see, to pass into it, to receive it into ourselves, to bathe in it, to become part of it."[2]

The legacy of beauty we're longing to have and to leave—in ourselves and in our families—ultimately comes through brokenness. Well acquainted with grief as a man who lost his wife, child, and mother in a horrific auto accident, Jerry Sittser wrote the book *A Grace Disguised* to process God's presence in his grief. Nearly twenty years later he revisits his learning in *A Grace Revealed*, discovering that grace disguised today can be grace revealed tomorrow. "[God] wants to use the harsh conditions of life to shape us—and eventually the whole world—into something extraordinarily beautiful."[3]

I'm holding on to two sentences. I hold them out to you.

Sentence Number One: *God loves the broken.* He loves broken families—and the broken people within them. Truly. Enough to die for us.

God loves us so much that he won't leave us the way we are but rather he continually re-forms us into who he means for us to be *through* brokenness. Sittser describes this process in the familiar theological term *redemption.* "Redemption is rooted in a paradox, which can be summed up in a simple phrase: we become who we already are in Jesus Christ."[4]

Take me. I'm not the same person I was. I'm not the same person I was at five when my dad told me he was divorcing my mom and leaving me. I'm not the same person I was at eleven, when I turned off my mom's alarm and tried to wake her up. I'm not the same person I was when I asked Jesus to live in my heart at sixteen. Or when I found out my brother was gay. Or when I got married. Or when I adopted my daughter and then my son. Or when I became a grandmother the first time—or the second.

I'm not the same person I was when I started writing this book several months ago. And I know now that I won't be the same person when this manuscript is released to others to read.

I'm broken.

The pieces of me don't go back together the way they once did. Oh, some fit still. I find my giggle as I lap through the family room to the kitchen to the living room, chasing my grandson. I enliven discussions on strategy and vision and ministry dreams. I open my heart to welcome others to explore Jesus with me in relationship.

But I am different. In most conversations, I leave answers off the table and, in their place, I raise my hand with questions. I nod and slide my arm around a wounded one. I entertain certainty in someone who hasn't had enough life to be certain of anything yet. I've learned how very much I don't know.

I'm broken. God loves broken me. And he is re-forming (redeeming) me, making me over into another version of me through brokenness.

A while back—maybe five or six years ago—I began to hear God nudging me with another one of his "utterances" in my days. I had no clue what he meant but I kept hearing, *I am forming that to which I've already called you.* Okay.

At first I thought he was talking about MOPS: that God was forming MOPS International in some new way and that I would be called to some role with it. So I pursued strategies and goals to reach moms with the help and hope of Jesus. Gradually, God made it clear that he was forming MOPS and me to go in different directions—that he was "uncalling" me to MOPS and calling me to something else.

I had no idea what it was that would be my "next."

My mind stretched in search of answers for a long time. Where did I *belong*? Who was I without the mantle of MOPS? (I now refer to this season as the *dis-mantling* of Elisa.) Finally, backed into a corner in a conversation with a friend, I received her probing reflection. "There seems to be a desperation about you right now, Elisa. It's like you're determined to *attach* to someone or something."

I am forming that to which I've already called you.

Attach yourself to me.

The phrases followed each other, weaving together a new place to be in the shaping of a new person to be. A calling: to be me. Sound familiar? "If anyone belongs to Christ, there is a new creation. The old things have gone; everything is made new!" (2 Corinthians 5:17). While no doubt Paul is referring to the old sin nature that used to hold us captive but no longer does when we are in Christ, he is also alluding to the "new" that God re-forms/redeems in us through our death to ourselves. Through our brokenness.

God loves the broken. One sentence starts and ends my day: *I love you, Elisa.* Period. I am loved. I lay down my straining to fix what is broken around me, my hunger for something more perfect than I can produce. I sit with the shards of my very imperfect life, surer than ever that the pieces simply cannot be put back together again—at least not in the same way as before. God reforms me.

The same is true for my broken family. God loves Evan and he is re-forming him. God loves Eva and is re-forming her. God loves Ethan and is re-forming him. God loves my brother and my sister and my grandson and my son-in-law. He is re-forming them all through brokenness.

And the very same is true for broken you and your broken family. God loves you and your family, and he will re-form you and your family through brokenness. You may not see it at this very minute. You may only be able to see the pile of shattered hopes and plans strewn about you on the floor. You may experience a long season of separation from the family member you so long to love. You may never see reconciliation this side of heaven. You may see steps stuttering to and from hope and help with very little visible progress. But God loves broken you and he will re-form broken you into his best idea for you.

Roy Hession writes, "To be broken is the beginning of revival."[5] And redemption. And re-formation. God loves the broken: broken families and the broken people in them.

Sentence Number Two: *God uses the broken.* He uses broken families—and the broken people in them. God uses this "re-formed" me as he raises me up to be strangely even more effective through my brokenness. God uses my family—as a whole in this world and each broken member of it. This is not a new concept with God. Decades ago, M. R. DeHaan of Radio Bible Class tracked the theme of brokenness through Scripture:

- God used two broken stone tablets to cause the Israelites to repent of their disobedience.
- God used broken earthen vessels (pitchers that covered torches) to give the impression of an enormous army accompanying Gideon and to cause his enemies to pull back in dread.
- God used a broken heart to return King David to himself.
- God used a broken roof to provide access for a cripple to be lowered by four faithful friends into the healing presence of Jesus.
- God used broken loaves to feed five thousand and then some.
- God used broken fishing nets to challenge the disciples to depend on him rather than their own efforts for their needs.
- God used a broken flask of nard to express the love that flows out of a relationship with him.

- God used a broken ship to steer Paul to the island of Malta to reveal the gospel to the natives there.
- God used a broken body, pierced for our sins, to provide salvation for all humankind.[6]

God uses the broken. It's hard—at first—to understand. Isn't it? Brokenness doesn't disqualify us. Brokenness placed in God's hands to redeem and re-form can actually qualify us for life and love and even leadership.

Dean Merrill writes of a visit he took to a port city on Lake Michigan and what he saw there:

> My host took me . . . to see the harbor area. A lake freighter nearly a block long was tied up, and I stared at the gaping hole in its side that ran from bow to stern, several feet wide. "What's happening?" I asked. "Why is there such a huge cut along the ship?"
>
> "They've brought her in here to overhaul her, actually to enlarge her capacity," was the reply. "They have literally sliced the thing right through the middle, jacked up the top half, and now they're welding in pieces to fill the space. When they're done, the ship will carry almost twice as much cargo as before."[7]

Luci Shaw uses the metaphor of light to eloquently express our broken suffering in our world:

> *Each day he seems to shine*
> *from the more primitive pots*
> *the battered bowls*
>
> *Service may polish silver &*
> *gold up to honor*

& I could cry to glitter
like porcelain
or lead crystal

But light is a clearer
contrast through my cracks
& flame is cleaner seen
if its container
does not compete[8]

Long before Luci penned her poem, the apostle Paul wrote, "We have this treasure from God, but we are like clay jars that hold the treasure. This shows that the great power is from God, not from us" (2 Corinthians 4:7).

There's no such thing as a perfect family. But God loves the broken. You. Me. Us. God uses the broken. You. Me. Our families.

I come from a broken family, and despite my best efforts to create a perfect family of my own, I still come from a broken family. So do you.

Thank God.

Because there is beauty in the broken.

....

When you have no experience of pain, it is rather hard to experience joy.

—PHILIP YANCEY[9]

If I Knew Then . . .

If I knew then what I know now, would I have had children?

It's taken years for me to gather the courage to ask this question. It seems such a barbaric betrayal for a mother's mind.

On the one hand I answer, *Of course!* My children—and their children—have defined my days with joy and depth. They are the center of holiday celebrations, the motivation of my everyday efforts, the legacy of my life. They have been my *world*.

Even with unexpected turns resulting in today's realities, I still answer *of course!* In the "then" of my twenties I was idealistic enough to believe that I could love any child through whatever they were facing in such a way that they would never have to face it again. I saw myself as healer and wound-mender and launcher-beyond-all-struggle.

On the other hand . . . I wonder. I never expected the potholes lining my motherhood path. The heart-stretching, gut-wrenching, shoulder-drooping pain. The stunning surprises, one devastation after another. The disappointments—are we *allowed* to be disappointed with our children? The money sunk into fixing the messes. The energy invested. The sleepless nights. The weightiness of it all.

I didn't know that then.

Our dear friend Philip wrote to Evan and me, "Your hearts sound so heavy, so wounded. I read the Psalms and think of you. So many parents ask, 'Is it worth it? Would I do it again?' God, with a heart wounded six billion times, always answers, 'Yes.'"

I didn't know then what I do know now: that every child's journey is his or her own. God is guiding and shaping their individual lives and the lives they individually influence. No parent, no matter how dedicated, expert, present, and loving, can produce a perfectly healthy and happy adult. Such a feat is simply not within our power. At the same time, every parent is divinely used to affect the journey of every child—toward this and away from that, even if with opposite-from-intended results. ("If you say don't go there, there I will tread!" "If you say head over here, I will head over there!")

And I didn't know then what I do know now: that every child of every parent is God's instrument in the life of his or her parent. My children have been God's chief tool for the shaping of *me*, shaving off the certainty, molding a softer version, raising up the gumption necessary to face another day.

Evidently, my children needed me—who I thought I was and who I've become—to mold their beings. And certainly, I needed them—who they were and weren't, who they are and aren't, who they will be and won't be—to become who I was, am, and will be.

Appendix of Hope

The holes in our lives can become places of hope.
—LANA BATEMAN[1]

What Can I Believe?

O God, I am so fragile:
    my dreams get broken,
    my relationships get broken,
    my heart gets broken,
    my body gets broken.

What can I believe,
    except that you will not despise a broken heart,
    that old and broken people shall yet dream dreams,
    and that the lame shall leap for joy,
        the blind see,
            the deaf hear.

What can I believe,
    except what Jesus taught:

that only what is first broken, like bread,
    can be shared;
that only what is broken
    is open to your entry;
that old wineskins must be ripped open and replaced
    if the wine of new life is to expand....

—Ted Loder[2]

He Giveth More Grace

He giveth more grace as the burdens grow greater,
He sendeth more strength when the labors increase;
To added affliction He addeth His mercy,
To multiplied trials, His multiplied peace.
When we have exhausted our store of endurance,
When our strength has failed ere the day is half done,
When we reach the end of our hoarded resources,
Our Father's full giving is only begun.
His love has no limit,
His grace has no measure,
His power has no boundary known unto men;
For out of His infinite riches in Jesus,
He giveth and giveth and giveth again!

—Annie Johnson Flint[3]

St. Patrick's Breastplate

I arise today
Through the strength of heaven:
Light of sun,
Radiance of moon,

Splendour of fire,
Speed of lightening,
Swiftness of wind,
Depth of sea,
Stability of earth,
Firmness of rock.

I arise today
Through God's strength to pilot me:
God's might to uphold me,
God's wisdom to guide me,
God's eye to look before me,
God's ear to hear me,
God's word to speak for me,
God's hand to guard me,
God's way to lie before me,
God's shield to protect me,
God's host to save me
From snares of devils,
From temptations of vices,
From every one who shall wish me ill,
Afar and anear,
Alone and in a multitude.
Christ to shield me today
Against poison, against burning,
Against drowning, against wounding,
So that there may come to me abundance of reward.
Christ with me, Christ before me, Christ behind me,
Christ in me, Christ beneath me, Christ above me,
Christ on my right, Christ on my left,
  Christ when I lie down, Christ when I sit down, Christ
      when I arise,
Christ in the heart of every man who thinks of me,

Christ in the mouth of every one who speaks of me,
Christ in every eye that sees me,
Christ in every ear that hears me.

I arise today
Through a mighty strength, the invocation of the Trinity,
Through belief in the threeness,
Through confession of the oneness
Of the Creator of Creation.

—St. Patrick[4]

Prodigals

Most of us have prayed for years that God would change our prodigals. Perhaps we need to pray that God will change us first. Perhaps God wants to work on our bitterness, and give us the grace to forgive. Maybe God wants to ease our pain by having us confront our grief and disappointment. Maybe God wants to deflate our sense of self-righteousness and remind us that He is God, not us. Maybe God wants to replace our hopelessness with joy and thankfulness.

Our prodigals surely need the touch of God, but perhaps we need to feel it first. Then, as God works His kindness and healing in our hearts, our faces and our words can better reflect God's love to our prodigals and to everyone else around us.

—Phil Waldrep and Pat Sprinkle[5]

Christmas Wishes

I'm sitting in a mall listening to Christmas music. It is, of course, that most innocuous sort of Christmas music that is designed not to offend anyone. I call it "Santa Happy Joy Joy" music. It is insipid.

We have a problem. We all love Christmas. Especially commercial interests like malls and retailers who see a huge spike in their sales every December. So we want to celebrate Christmas and the fiscal blessings it brings. But we don't know what to celebrate. Christmas is, at its core, a religious holiday, which of course makes us uncomfortable as we all try to prevent anyone from feeling left out. So we write Christmas music and Christmas movies and TV shows that feel like they're about something, but they really aren't. Like a parade or a fireworks show at Disneyland. It FEELS important. The music SOUNDS like meaningful values are being discussed—like the secret to true joy has been discovered and is now being disseminated and celebrated. It sounds, dare I say, almost religious. But it isn't. Modern Christmas music and TV shows have nothing to say. Nothing to celebrate. So we celebrate the "holiday spirit" and "good tidings." We celebrate celebration.

Is it any wonder so many people report feeling depressed at this time of year? Modern Christmas is a sham. A false front. It's covered with lights and tinsel and holly, but when you open the door and look inside, there's nothing there.

"There's FAMILY! Modern Christmas celebrates family!" Sure, many Christmas songs and TV shows seem to conclude that the real joy of the season is the time spent with family. And that might sometimes be the case. But in a fallen world, "family" is fallen, too. Many don't have families. Many more have families that don't function—circumstances that make the idea of large family gatherings far from exciting.

My parents split up when I was nine years old, and thereafter the idea of family, for me anyway, was filled with negative emotion. In college friends would ask if I was going to have Christmas with my family. "I'm going to my mom's," I'd say, or "I'm going to my dad's." But where exactly was my family—that romantic ideal from the Christmas songs and TV shows? I had no clue. It had simply vanished.

So I have a bit of a problem with our nationalized, commercialized, secular Christmas. It's a joke. The transcendent value it celebrates—family—is as broken as the rest of this fallen world.

But there was a time, not too terribly long ago, when Christmas celebrated something truly transcendent—something that could transcend all of the world's brokenness. The birth of someone "from beyond." Beyond our brokenness. Someone who carried within them the ability to make us whole.

And so we wrote songs and we sang them from hearts filled with joy. Real joy. We celebrated a savior. Someone who can make us whole. Who can mend the pieces of a broken world. Someone WORTH celebrating.

So this Christmas, don't pretend. Don't pretend joy can be found simply by saying the word over and over. Don't pretend "merry" is a decoration, like cake frosting, that can be spread liberally across our lives. Don't pretend peace and deep happiness can be achieved through a perfectly planned and executed family gathering. Because they can't. Broken, broken, broken. All is broken. Nothing works quite right—even when wrapped in twinkling, low-voltage LED lights.

We need a savior. And 2000 years ago, we got one. So this Christmas, celebrate what really matters.

—Phil Vischer[6]

Father, Hear Us

Father, hear us, we are praying,
Hear the words our hearts are saying,
We are praying for our children.

Keep them from the powers of evil,
From the secret, hidden peril,
Father, hear us for our children.

From the whirlpool that would suck them,
From the treacherous quicksand, pluck them,
Father, hear us for our children.

From the worldling's hollow gladness,
From the sting of faithless sadness,
Father, Father, keep our children.

Through life's troubled waters steer them,
Through life's bitter battle cheer them,
Father, Father, be Thou near them.

Read the language of our longing,
Read the worldless pleadings thronging,
Holy Father, for our children.

And wherever they may bide,
Lead them Home at eventide.

—Amy Carmichael[7]

The Serenity Prayer

God grant me the serenity
to accept the things I cannot change;
courage to change the things I can;
and wisdom to know the difference.

Living one day at a time;
Enjoying one moment at a time;
Accepting hardships as the pathway to peace;
Taking, as He did, this sinful world
as it is, not as I would have it;
Trusting that He will make all things right
if I surrender to His Will;
That I may be reasonably happy in this life
and supremely happy with Him
Forever in the next.
Amen.

—Reinhold Niebuhr[8]

Biblical Quitting

Biblical *quitting* goes hand in hand with *choosing*. When we quit those things that are damaging to our souls, or the souls of others, we are freed up to choose other ways of being and relating that are rooted in love and lead to life. For example . . .

When we *quit* fear of what others think, we *choose* freedom.
When we *quit* lies, we *choose* truth.
When we *quit* blaming, we *choose* to take responsibility.
When we *quit* faulty thinking, we *choose* to live in reality.

—Geri and Peter Scazzero[9]

Am I a Proud or a Broken Person?
Am I? How Can We Know?

Attitudes Toward Others

Proud people focus on the failures of others and can readily point out those faults.

Broken people are more conscious of their own spiritual need than of anyone else's. . . .

ATTITUDES ABOUT RIGHTS

Proud people have to prove that they are right—they have to get the last word.

Broken people are willing to yield the right to be right. . . .

ATTITUDES ABOUT SERVICE AND MINISTRY

Proud people desire to be served—they want life to revolve around them and their own needs.

Broken people are motivated to serve others and to be sure others' needs are met before their own. . . .

ATTITUDES ABOUT RECOGNITION

Proud people crave self-advancement.

Broken people desire to promote others. . . .

ATTITUDES ABOUT THEMSELVES

Proud people feel confident in how much they know. . . .

Broken people are humbled by how very much they have to learn. . . .

ATTITUDES ABOUT RELATIONSHIPS

Proud people keep others at arms' length.

Broken people are willing to risk getting close to others and to take risks of loving intimately. . . .

ATTITUDES ABOUT SIN

Proud people want to be sure that no one finds out when they have sinned; their instinct is to cover up.

Broken people aren't overly concerned with who knows or who finds out about their sin—they are willing to be exposed because they have nothing to lose. . . .

Attitudes About Their Walk With God

Proud people are blind to the true condition of their hearts. *Broken people walk in the light and acknowledge the truth about their lives.*

—Nancy Leigh DeMoss[10]

In His Image

The portion of human anatomy I have specialized in is that marvelous creation the hand....

I know what crucifixion must do to a human hand.

Executioners of that day drove their spikes through the wrist, right through the carpal tunnel that houses finger-controlling tendons and the median nerve. It is impossible to force a spike there without crippling the hand into a claw shape. Jesus had no anesthetic. He allowed those hands to be marred and crippled and destroyed.

Later, His weight hung from them, tearing more tissue, releasing more blood. There could be no more helpless image than that of a God hanging paralyzed from a tree....

But that is not the last glimpse we have of Jesus' hands in the biblical record. He appears again, in a closed room, where Thomas is still doubting the unlikely story he thinks his friends have concocted. People do not rise from the dead, he scoffs. It must have been a ghost, or an illusion. At that moment, Jesus holds up those unmistakable hands His disciples had seen perform miracles. The scars give proof that they belong to him, the One who had died on the cross. The body has changed—it can pass through walls and locked doors to join them. But the scars remain. Jesus invites Thomas to come and trace them with his own fingers....

Why did Christ keep His scars? He could have had a perfect body, or no body, when He returned to splendor in heaven. Instead he carried with Him remembrances of His visit to earth. For a reminder of His time here, He chose scars. That is why I say God hears and understands our pain, and even absorbs it into Himself—because He kept those scars as a lasting image of wounded humanity. He has been here; He has borne the sentence. The pain of man has become the pain of God.

—Dr. Paul Brand and Philip Yancey[11]

Broken Shells

During my most recent outing to the beach, I was looking for a shell for a friend going through a difficult time, a friend who also loves beaches. I used the time on the beach to pray for her and her family in the valley. I was very frustrated, because I kept finding broken shells, but couldn't find a complete, whole, "perfect" shell. So I started picking up broken shells, thinking that I could sort and discard at the end of my walk.

Then I looked at the gravel on the beach and noticed what I have always known: that the beach "sand" is actually comprised of tiny shards of broken shells. Our lives are like the shells. We get tumbled about in life and start exposing cracks and gaps in our shells, until eventually we are just crushed into the fabric of our surroundings. How depressing. Is that all the meaning we have, to become a grain of sand underfoot?

The Bible contains this concept; in the fall of humans, we are reminded that we are created from dust and we will return to dust.

Eventually I found a whole, complete, "perfect" shell to slip into my pocket, but at the end of my walk, I kept the broken shells.

Because both are valuable I don't want to neatly and quickly resolve my wondering about the forces that seem to crush us in life. My view of God and redemption is strong enough and also open enough to allow me to question the reason for crushing and to rail at the injustice of such pain. I can also hope, for my friend and myself, for a season of beauty rather than crushing. Meanwhile, both the complete and the broken shell remind me of the process of life and redemption.

—CARLA FOOTE[12]

Scriptures of Hope

The LORD is close to the brokenhearted,
and he saves those whose spirits have been crushed.

—PSALM 34:18

He heals the brokenhearted
and bandages their wounds.

—PSALM 147:3

He has made everything beautiful in its time. Also He has put eternity in their hearts, except that no one can find out the work that God does from beginning to end.

—ECCLESIASTES 3:11 NKJV

The Spirit of the Lord GOD is upon Me,
Because the LORD has anointed Me
To preach good tidings to the poor;
He has sent Me to heal the brokenhearted,
To proclaim liberty to the captives,
And the opening of the prison to those who are bound;

To proclaim the acceptable year of the Lord,
And the day of vengeance of our God;
To comfort all who mourn,
To console those who mourn in Zion,
To give them beauty for ashes,
The oil of joy for mourning,
The garment of praise for the spirit of heaviness;
That they may be called trees of righteousness,
The planting of the Lord, that He may be glorified.

—Isaiah 61:1–3 nkjv

The sacrifice God wants is a broken spirit.
God, you will not reject a heart that is broken and sorry
for sin.

—Psalm 51:17

I find rest in God;
only he gives me hope.

—Psalm 62:5

But the people who trust the Lord will become strong again.
They will rise up as an eagle in the sky;
they will run and not need rest;
they will walk and not become tired.

—Isaiah 40:31

We also have joy with our troubles, because we know that
these troubles produce patience. And patience produces

character, and character produces hope. And this hope will never disappoint us, because God has poured out his love to fill our hearts. He gave us his love through the Holy Spirit, whom God has given to us.

—ROMANS 5:3–5

Look at the new thing I am going to do.
    It is already happening. Don't you see it?
I will make a road in the desert
    and rivers in the dry land.

—ISAIAH 43:19

I know that my Defender lives,
    and in the end he will stand upon the earth.

—JOB 19:25

Those who look to him are radiant;
    their faces are never covered with shame.

—PSALM 34:5 NIV

Godly sorrow brings repentance that leads to salvation and leaves no regret, but worldly sorrow brings death.

—2 CORINTHIANS 7:10 NIV

I leave you peace; my peace I give you. I do not give it to you as the world does. So don't let your hearts be troubled or afraid.

— JOHN 14:27

I told you these things so that you can have peace in me. In this
world you will have trouble, but be brave! I have defeated the
world.

—John 16:33

Do not worry about anything, but pray and ask God for
everything you need, always giving thanks. And God's peace,
which is so great we cannot understand it, will keep your
hearts and minds in Christ Jesus.

—Philippians 4:6–7

Love never gives up.
Love cares more for others than for self.
Love doesn't want what it doesn't have.
Love doesn't strut,
Doesn't have a swelled head,
Doesn't force itself on others,
Isn't always "me first,"
Doesn't fly off the handle,
Doesn't keep score of the sins of others,
Doesn't revel when others grovel,
Takes pleasure in the flowering of truth,
Puts up with anything,
Trusts God always,
Always looks for the best,
Never looks back,
But keeps going to the end.
Love never dies.

—1 Corinthians 13: 4–8 msg

Notes

IT'S TIME TO TALK
1. Frederick Buechner, *Telling Secrets* (New York: HarperCollins, 1992), 3.
2. Brennan Manning, *The Rabbi's Heartbeat* (Colorado Springs: NavPress, 2003), 13.

PART ONE: BROKEN US
1. Glòria T. Delamar, "Ring-a-round a Rosie," *Mother Goose, From Nursery to Literature* (Lincoln: iUniverse.com, 2001), 38.
2. Richard Rohr, *Falling Upward* (San Francisco: Jossey-Bass, 2011), iBook, 24.

CHAPTER 1: I COME FROM A BROKEN FAMILY
1. Ann VosKamp, *One Thousand Gifts* (Grand Rapids: Zondervan, 2010), 175.

CHAPTER 2: OUR BROKEN FAMILIES
1. Peg Tyre, "Lesson Plan for an A+ Parent: 7 Ways to Help Your Children Achieve Their Best," *USA Weekend*, August 10–12, 2012, 1.
2. Rainbows, "A Generation at Risk," Statistics; http://www.rainbows .org/statistics.html.
3. Merriam-Webster Online Dictionary, s.v. "broken"; http://www .merriam-webster.com/dictionary/broken. The Free Online

Dictionary, Thesaurus and Encyclopedia, s.v., "broken"; http://www
.thefreedictionary.com/broken.

4. Rainbows, "A Generation at Risk."

5. Tim Chen, "American Household Credit Card Debt Statistics through
   2012," January 8, 2012, NerdWallet.com; http://www.nerdwallet.com
   /blog/credit-card-data/average-credit-card-debt-household/.

6. David Kinnaman, "The State of the Evangelical Church," speech at
   Christian Leadership Alliance CEO Forum, April 23, 2008.

7. David Kinnaman, *You Lost Me* (Grand Rapids: Baker, 2011), iBook, 19.

8. Sharon Begley, "But I Did Everything Right!" *Newsweek*, Summer 2008.

9. "A Piece of Furniture," *Juno*, directed by Jason Reitman (2007, Fox
   Home Entertainment, April 15, 2008), DVD.

10. Amy Martin, "Losing Church: My Slow Journey to the Margins,"
    March 23, 2012; http://amydmartin.wordpress.com/2012/03/23/
    church-in-pieces/.

11. Brene Brown, "The Power of Vulnerability," June 2010, TED.com;
    http://www.ted.com/talks/brene_brown_on_vulnerability.html.

12. Brene Brown, *I Thought It Was Just Me (But It Isn't)* (New York: Gotham,
    2007), iBook, 188.

13. Leslie Leyland Fields, "The Myth of the Perfect Parent," *Christianity
    Today*, January 2010, 27.

Chapter 3: God's Broken Family

1. Barbara Brown Taylor, *An Altar in the World* (New York: HarperOne,
   2009), 157–58.

2. Robert Gelinas, "Transfiguration: Beautiful," sermon at Colorado
   Community Church, May 13, 2012; http://www.coloradocommunity
   .org/media/sermons/sermons-online/?page=4.

3. Strong's Hebrew Lexicon, 2250; http://www.eliyah.com/cgi-bin
   /strongs.cgi?file=hebrewlexicon&isindex=2250; R. Jamieson, A. R.
   Fausset & D. Brown, *Commentary Critical and Explanatory of the Whole
   Bible* (Oak Habor, WA: Logos Research Systems, Inc., 1997), Isaiah
   53:5; J. F. Walvoord and R. B. Zuck, Dallas Theological Seminary
   (1985). *The Bible Knowledge Commentary: An Exposition of the Scriptures*
   (Wheaton, IL: Victor Books, 1985), Isaiah 53:5.

4. Strong's Hebrew Lexicon, 7495; http://www.eliyah.com/cgi-bin
   /strongs.cgi?file=hebrewlexicon&isindex=7495; Victoria Neufeldt,
   David B. Guralnik, Eds., *Third College Edition Webster's Dictionary*,
   (New York: Prentice Hall, 1986), 621.

5. Brennan Manning, *The Ragamuffin Gospel* (Sisters, OR: Multnomah, 1990), 86.

PART TWO: BROKEN FAMILY VALUES

1. Brennan Mannig, *Ruthless Trust* (New York: HarperCollins, 2000), 48.

CHAPTER 4: COMMITMENT

1. Weston Gentry, "Colorado Families Celebrate Newest Family Members at Adoption Proceedings," *The Denver Post*, November 20, 2011, DenverPost.com; http://www.denverpost.com/news /ci_19375892.
2. Thomas Merton, *Thoughts in Solitude* (New York: Farrar, Straus and Giroux, 1999), part 2, chapter 2.

CHAPTER 5: HUMILITY

1. Brennan Manning, *The Ragamuffin Gospel* (Sisters, OR: Multnomah, 1990), 74.
2. Ibid., 181.
3. Ibid., 132.
4. Richard Rohr, *Falling Upward* (San Francisco: Jossey-Bass, 2011), iBook, 73.
5. Alice Miller, *The Drama of the Gifted Child* (New York: Basic Books, 1981), vii–xv.
6. Anne Lamott, *Traveling Mercies* (New York: Pantheon, 1999), 143.
7. Steve and Valerie Bell, *Made to Be Loved* (Chicago: Moody, 1999).
8. Robert Gelinas, "Grace-Centered Living Part 2," sermon at Colorado Community Church, February 26, 2012; http://www .coloradocommunity.org/media/sermons/sermons-online/?page=6.
9. Richard Rohr, *Falling Upward* (San Francisco: Jossey-Bass, 2011), iBook, 86.

CHAPTER 6: COURAGE

1. Tina Griego, "From a Family's Tragedy Comes Lessons in Humility," *The Denver Post*, November 27, 2011, 6B.
2. Sue Monk Kidd, *The Dance of the Dissident Daughter* (San Francisco: HarperSanFrancisco, 1992), 23.
3. John Eldredge, *Wild at Heart* (Nashville: Thomas Nelson, 2001), 32.
4. Abraham Verghese, *Cutting for Stone* (New York: Vintage, 2009), iBook, 801.

CHAPTER 7: REALITY

1. Philip Yancey, *Reaching for the Invisible God* (Grand Rapids: Zondervan, 2000), 194.
2. Sarah Young, *Jesus Calling* (Nashville: Thomas Nelson, 2004), July 28.

CHAPTER 8: RELINQUISHMENT

1. Sarah Young, *Jesus Calling* (Nashville: Thomas Nelson, 2004), August 23.
2. Laura Schroff, *An Invisible Thread* (New York: Howard, 2011), 311.
3. Roy Hession, *The Calvary Road* (Fort Washington, PA: Christian Literature Crusade, 1990), 23, 25.

CHAPTER 9: DIVERSITY

1. "Brad Pitt's Brother on Viral Ad: 'It's Surreal,'" Matt Lauer, *The Today Show*, NBC, July 9, 2012; http://video.today.msnbc.msn.com/today/48118432#48118432.
2. Brenda tells her story in Brenda Warner and Jennifer Schuchmann, *One Call Away* (Nashville: Thomas Nelson, 2011).
3. Miroslav Volf, *Exclusion and Embrace* (Nashville: Abingdon, 1996), 20.
4. Brennan Manning, *The Relentless Tenderness of Jesus* (Grand Rapids: Baker, 2004), 24.

CHAPTER 10: PARTNERSHIP

1. Joan Anderson, *An Unfinished Marriage* (New York: Broadway Books, 2002), 8.
2. Frederick Buechner, *The Sacred Journey* (New York: HarperCollins, 1982), 46.

CHAPTER 11: FAITH

1. Todd Burpo, *Heaven Is for Real* (Nashville: Thomas Nelson, 2010), 72.
2. Eugene Peterson, *Living the Message* (New York: HarperCollins, 1996), 290.
3. Sarah Young, *Jesus Calling* (Nashville: Thomas Nelson, 2004), July 27.

CHAPTER 12: LOVE

1. Scene 4, *Best Exotic Marigold Hotel*, directed by John Madden (2011; Beverly Hills, CA: Twentieth Century Fox Home Entertainment, 2012), DVD.

2. Judith Viorst, *Necessary Losses* (New York: Fawcett Gold Medal, 1986), 2–3.

3. Oswald Chambers, *The Love of God* (Grand Rapids: Discovery House, 1988), 17.

CHAPTER 13: RESPECT

1. Brene Brown, *I Thought it Was Just Me (But It Isn't)* (New York: Gotham, 2007), iBook, 344.

2. Annie Dillard, *Teaching a Stone to Talk: Expeditions and Encounters* (New York: Harper & Row, 1982), 40–41.

3. Robert A. J. Gagnon, *The Bible and Homosexual Practice: Text and Hermeneutics* (Nashville: Abingdon, 2001), 185–228.

4. Todd Morrison, "Can I Come to Your Church? I'm Gay." *Relevant Magazine*, May 24, 2012; http://www.relevantmagazine.com/god /church/blog/29292-qcan-i-come-to-your-church-im-gayq.

5. Sarah Young, *Jesus Calling* (Nashville: Thomas Nelson, 2004), January 18.

6. Donald Miller, *Blue Like Jazz* (Nashville: Thomas Nelson, 2003), 146.

CHAPTER 14: FORGIVENESS

1. C. S. Lewis, *The Business of Heaven* (San Diego: Harcourt Brace Jovanovich, 1984), 62.

2. Laura Hillenbrand, *Unbroken* (New York: Random House, 2010), iBook, 574.

3. R. T. Kendall, *Total Forgiveness* (Lake Mary, FL: Charisma, 2002), 16.

4. Ibid., 75.

5. Richard Rohr, *Falling Upward* (San Francisco: Jossey-Bass, 2011), iBook, 83.

CHAPTER 15: THANKFULNESS

1. Ann Voskamp, speech at Extraordinary Women in Tupelo, MS, November 2011.

2. Sarah Young, *Jesus Calling* (Nashville: Thomas Nelson, 2004), July 24.

3. Frederick Buechner, *Godric* (New York: Atheneum, 1980; Harper & Row, 1983), 96.

PART THREE: THE BEAUTY OF BROKEN

1. Nikos Kazantzakis, *Report to Greco*, trans. P. A. Bien (New York: Simon and Schuster, 1965), 16.

CHAPTER 16: A BEAUTIFULLY BROKEN LEGACY

1. Crispin Sartwell, *Six Names of Beauty* (New York: Routledge, 2004), vii.
2. C. S. Lewis, *The Weight of Glory* (New York: HarperCollins, 1949, 1976), 42.
3. Jerry Sittser, *A Grace Revealed* (Grand Rapids: Zondervan, 2012), 19.
4. Ibid., 24.
5. Roy Hession, *The Calvary Road* (Fort Washington, PA: Christian Literature Crusade, 1990), 21.
6. Summarized from M.R. DeHaan, *Broken Things: Why We Suffer* (Grand Rapids: Discovery House, 1948).
7. Dean Merrill, *Another Chance* (Grand Rapids: Zondervan, 1982), 131.
8. Luci Shaw, "That the glory may be of God," *The Sighting* (Wheaton: Harold Shaw Publishers, 1981), 28.
9. Philip Yancey, *Where Is God When It Hurts?* (Grand Rapids: Zondervan, 1977; repr. 2009), Kindle edition, 47.

APPENDIX OF HOPE

1. Lana Bateman, prayer advocate for Women of Faith, in prayer offered at Hartford, CT, event on November 3, 2012.
2. Ted Loder, "What Can I Believe?" *Guerrillas of Grace* (Philadelphia: Innisfree Press, 1984), 58. Copyright © 1984, 2005 Ted Loder, admin. Augsburg Fortress. Reproduced by permission. All rights reserved.
3. Annie Johnson Flint, 1941. Renewed 1969 by Lillenas Publishing Co. Annie died in the 1930s after being bedridden most of her life due to severe rheumatoid arthritis.
4. St. Patrick, "St. Patrick's Breastplate," trans. Kuno Meyer, in *Irish Verse: An Anthology*, ed. Bob Blaisdell (Mineola, NY: Dover Publications, 2002), 3–4.
5. Phil Waldrep and Pat Sprinkle, *Parenting Prodigals* (Friendswood, TX: Baxter Press, 2001), 210–11.
6. Phil Vischer, "Christmas Wishes," Philvischer.com, December 5, 2012; http://www.philvischer.com/phil-news/christmas-wishes/.
7. Amy Carmichael, *Gold Cord* (London: Society for Promoting Christian Knowledge, 1932), 142. Amy never had children herself but was lovingly called *amma* (mother) by hundreds of Indian street children.
8. "Serenity Prayer," attributed to Reinhold Niebuhr.
9. Geri Scazzero and Peter Scazzero, *I Quit!* (Grand Rapids: Zondervan, 2010), 16.

10. Excerpted from Nancy DeMoss, *Brokenness: The Heart God Revives* (Chicago, IL: Moody Press, 2002), 88–101.
11. Dr. Paul Brand and Philip Yancey, *In His Image* (Grand Rapids: Zondervan, 1984), 290–91.
12. Carla Foote, personal letter to the author, March 2011. Used by permission.

Acknowledgments

The credits roll. I stay in my seat to watch and take each name into my soul. These are those who have shaped my story. They need to be recognized. And thanked.

As I watch their names scroll across the screen of my life, I mouth the words: *thank you.*

To my publishing advocates:

Lee Hough: you listened and advocated and rewrote and refused to let me be anything different than who I am.

Rick Christian: You have always been in my corner.

Debbie Wickwire: You "got" me. And you made sure I brought me—all of me—forward.

Matt Baugher: You invested to make sure my story would connect with the stories of others, as many as possible, providing a bridge of hope.

Jennifer Stair: You spit-polished my words!

Meaghan Porter: You fine-printed my sources to perfection!

The whole Baugher team: Matt, Debbie, Meaghan, Emily, Stephanie, Kristi, Caroline, Andrea, Julie: You welcomed me, absorbed my offering and exhorted me to share—*unashamed.*

To those who lived my story alongside me, holding up my arms, walking down blind alleys, sharing their extra strength when I had none:

Carol, Karen P, Janis, Carla F, Georgia, Cyndi, Beth F, Liz, Craig, Karen M, Cheryl, Michele, Shelly, Janell, TJ, Meredith, Chris, Kim, Janene, Alexandra, Jackie, Beth L, Colin, Janella, Kendall, Naomi, Karen S, Corinne, Kenna, Tim, Alisha, Bonnie, Cindy P, Robert, Steve, Ali, Ketty, Soozi, my "bosses": Bob and Linda and Valerie and *all* at MOPS International.

My dear Covenant Sisters: Donna, Ellen, Judie, Linda, Rachael, Ruth and Verna.

The Fabs: Carla S, Cindy S, Debbie, J'Anne.

My "group": Ken and Diane, Philip and Janet, Chap and Dee, Chuck and Soozi, Larry and Rachael.

My Neighborhood Bible Study: Jane, Jen, Laura H, Laura T, Mary, Stacey, Suzanne.

New friends who have begun the journey with me: Marilyn, Pat, Patsy, Hilary, Shayne and Lindsay.

To my families:

My first family—broken and beautiful. Because you lived, I live.

Munna and Bop, Paige, Terry, Mary, Jim and Karen, Jeff and Christy, Andy and Trisha, Tom and Lynda, Cathy and Kirby.

My second family, all who are with me and all who are not: Extended Morgans: Newlin and Rosa Lee, Newlin and Robin, Will and Sara. My Morgans: Evan, Eva and Jason, Ethan, Thomas and Marcus and Malachi and two unnamed lovely littles. I burst with love for you—each and every—just the way you are.

My pets, who nuzzled me in grief and joyed with me in the everyday: Lacy, Velvet, Whisper, Ella, Wilson, and Darla.

Thank you for your beauty in my broken.

About the Author

Photo: Janella Thaxton

Elisa Morgan was named by *Christianity Today* as one of the top fifty women influencing today's church and culture and is one of today's most sought-after authors, speakers, and leaders. She has authored more than fifteen books on mothering, spiritual formation, and evangelism, including *She Did What She Could: Five Words of Jesus That Will Change Your Life* and *The NIV Mom's Devotional Bible.*

For twenty years, Elisa Morgan served as CEO of MOPS International (www.mops.org). Under her leadership MOPS grew from 350 to over 4,000 groups throughout the United States and in thirty other countries, influencing over 100,000 moms every year. Elisa now serves as president emerita.

Elisa received a BS from the University of Texas and an MDiv from Denver Seminary. She served as the dean of women of Western Bible College (now Colorado Christian University) and on the board of ECFA (Evangelical Council for Financial Accountability). Currently she serves on the board of Denver Seminary. She is married to Evan (senior vice president of global ministry efforts for RBC Ministries) and has two grown children and one grandchild who live near her in Denver, Colorado.

As the publisher of *FullFill* (www.fullfill.org), a free digital magazine for women of all ages, stages, and callings, her current mission is to mobilize women to invest their influence in God's purposes.

Contact Elisa at www.elisamorgan.com.

Where does your voice fit?
Join today, it's FREE!
Welcome to
FullFill™
For women. For leaders. Online. Anytime.
A digital magazine complete with compelling articles, beautiful images and inspirational videos from Elisa Morgan.
FullFill™.org — created for women like you who are living out your influence to impact your world.
We speak your language! www.FullFill.org